RAND | NATIONAL DEFENSE RESEARCH INSTITUTE

Improving Implementation of the Department of Defense Leahy Law

Michael J. McNerney, Jonah Blank, Becca Wasser, Jeremy Boback, Alexander Stephenson

Prepared for Office of the Secretary of Defense

For more information on this publication, visit www.rand.org/t/RR1737

Library of Congress Cataloging-in-Publication Data is available for this publication.
ISBN: 978-0-8330-9696-8

Published by the RAND Corporation, Santa Monica, Calif.
© Copyright 2017 RAND Corporation
RAND® is a registered trademark.

Cover: U.S. Marine Corps photo by Cpl. Reece Lodder.

Support RAND
Make a tax-deductible charitable contribution at
www.rand.org/giving/contribute

www.rand.org

Preface

The U.S. Department of Defense (DoD) provides assistance to foreign defense organizations around the world to achieve common security goals. The "DoD Leahy law," a provision in annual defense appropriation acts and, more recently, in the Carl Levin and Howard P. "Buck" McKeon National Defense Authorization Act for Fiscal Year 2015 (10 U.S. Code 2249e), prohibits the use of DoD funds for any training, equipment, or other assistance for a unit of foreign security force if there is credible information that the unit has committed a gross violation of human rights. DoD and the Department of State have worked together closely on clear and consistent guidance for implementing this law, as well as a more rigorous process to manage the vetting of foreign security forces.

This report analyzes existing guidance and every step of the Leahy vetting process, in order to suggest ways DoD might strengthen implementation of the DoD Leahy law, in many cases requiring close collaboration with the Department of State. The report should help strengthen DoD's capacity and capability to implement the law effectively. The contents should be of interest to defense and foreign policy analysts with an interest in security cooperation and human rights.

This research was sponsored by the Deputy Assistant Secretary of Defense for Stability and Humanitarian Affairs and conducted within the International Security and Defense Policy Center of the RAND National Defense Research Institute, a federally funded research and development center sponsored by the Office of the Secretary of Defense, the Joint Staff, the Unified Combatant Commands, the

Navy, the Marine Corps, the defense agencies, and the defense Intelligence Community.

For more information on the RAND International Security and Defense Policy Center, see www.rand.org/nsrd/ndri/centers/isdp or contact the director (contact information is provided on the web page).

Contents

Figures and Tables

Figures

Tables

Summary

Protection of human rights is an essential American value—one enshrined in the Constitution and increasingly extended in foreign policy. One way Congress has extended this value to foreign policy is through the "Leahy laws" (named for their author, Sen. Patrick Leahy, D-Vt.). These laws prohibit the U.S. government from providing assistance or training to members of a unit of any nation's security forces that has perpetuated a gross violation of human rights with impunity. The process by which individuals are examined for possible human rights violations is referred to as *Leahy vetting*.

Department of Defense (DoD) officials recognize that the U.S. military is an institutional beneficiary of the Leahy laws. Before their enactment, human rights considerations in the conduct of security cooperation activities with partner nations was often ad hoc, subject to the ups and downs of congressional mood and unrelated geopolitical swings. Leahy vetting provides a framework for assessing the human rights component of security cooperation decisions.

Leahy vetting has two purposes: avoiding allocation of U.S. taxpayer dollars to human rights abusers and actively assisting security partners (through both positive incentives and the prospect of decreased engagement) to improve their human rights records through improved training, professionalism, and accountability.[1] The challenges of vetting about 180,000 foreign security force personnel each year are daunting, however, particularly as so many of them are in unstable or develop-

---

[1] According to Senator Patrick Leahy's (D-Vt.) remarks at the U.S. Institute of Peace, as reported in Linwood Ham, "Human Rights Violations: U.S. Foreign Aid Accountability and Prevention," Washington, D.C.: U.S. Institute of Peace, March 29, 2015.

ing countries. Since the enactment of the first piece of Leahy legislation in 1997, the process—with its many steps and detailed operating manuals—has functioned like an assembly line that has been upgraded several times even as it operates at full speed. The inherent challenges of improving a complex vetting process, combined with frequent turnover of U.S. officials at different steps in the process, have occasionally led to confusion, misperceptions, and erroneous information. In some instances, early problems have been fixed through subsequent procedural actions, but some stakeholders remain unaware of these improvements. In other cases, bureaucratic work-arounds intended to improve process efficiency may have created new challenges. Because Leahy vetting is intended to be a continually improving process, this report aims to highlight procedures that could benefit from genuine reexamination or wider employment of proven best practices.

This report examines Leahy vetting from a process standpoint to help DoD improve its role in the existing system and to build further capacity to implement the DoD Leahy law effectively, with transparency and accountability for results. The multistage Leahy process consists of submitting identification information on individuals and units and vetting through an online tracking system at U.S. embassies abroad before further vetting and status determination at Department of State (DoS) headquarters in Washington, D.C.

Altogether, the process is a joint DoD and DoS effort because there are vetting requirements for both Title 10– and Title 22–funded programs. However, since the program's inception, DoD has relied on DoS's vetting process, including its International Vetting and Security Tracking (INVEST) system, to vet proposed recipients of DoD training. Since 2014, this review has also included recipients of equipment and other assistance. DoD needs a clear picture of how the process works, where it works well, and what challenges need to be addressed. Accordingly, we have sought to answer the following questions, which are based on initial discussions with stakeholders and structured to capture the widest possible range of challenges for the Leahy vetting program:

- What are the procedural and policy challenges for Leahy vetting?
- What are the time lines for vetting?

- How clear is the scope for vetting; that is, is it clear which programs and activities require vetting and which do not?
- What information is used for vetting, and how is its credibility determined?
- Are current training and staffing resources for U.S. vetting efforts adequate?
- What issues does Leahy vetting raise for partner relationships?

To explore these questions, we developed a baseline understanding of DoD's current role in the Leahy vetting process and common perceptions of the process. While DoD is responsible for programs that fall under Title 10 authorities, we have provided a holistic view of the vetting process because stakeholders—including embassy-level and DoS vetters, DoD and DoS officials, and partner nations—deal with both Title 10 and Title 22 authorities. We then interviewed DoD and DoS Leahy vetters—primarily security cooperation officers and DoS civilians, respectively—both in Washington and at a sample of embassies; reviewed embassy-level Leahy vetting standard operating procedures; and analyzed INVEST data to identify best practices and areas for improvement. Finally, we developed recommendations for improving the process and its outcomes.

The following sections highlight the key vetting issues and our main findings and recommendations.

Vetting Issue Areas

Process and Policy Challenges and Best Practices

Many challenges derive from the fact that DoD needs to be a more equal partner at every level in the vetting process; many stakeholders do not perceive DoD to have sufficient involvement. Our research also identified challenges arising from a lack of standard vetting procedures, for example, with each embassy maintaining its own standard operating procedures.

Nevertheless, some best practices do appear to be evident at the embassy level for both DoD and DoS vetters. These include building relationships with other sections at the embassy and vetters at DoS headquarters, developing an internal coordination mechanism, pro-actively managing requests for vetting, and streamlining processes to obtain partner-nation information.

Leahy cases that are suspended and canceled also pose challenges. INVEST data indicate one of four possible outcomes for each case: approval, rejection, suspension, or cancellation. From 2011 to 2015, almost 90 percent of all cases received approval. These numbers have been consistent in recent years, and stakeholder efforts to meet required deadlines are impressive, given the large number of cases that are sub-mitted late, i.e., within ten days before a decision is needed. Rejec-tion, which results in the withholding of training or assistance, occurs rarely. In our dataset, the average rejection rate was 0.3 percent per year. Cases are suspended when there is potential derogatory infor-mation related to individuals or units but DoS's Bureau of Democ-racy, Human Rights and Labor and the relevant regional bureau—often without DoD input—cannot agree on whether the information is credible or warrants a rejection. Cases are canceled for administrative reasons, such as when insufficient or non-specific vetting information is submitted and post does not provide the missing information before the start of training. The number of individuals and units whose cases were left unresolved—approximately 9 percent of cases were either sus-pended or canceled—pose challenges to both DoD planners and their foreign partners.

Regarding remediation, the process in which U.S. officials work with partner nations to help them take corrective action to address human rights violations, many interviewees expressed reluctance to undertake the remediation process, which they perceived as daunting.

Rather than being able to focus on long-term policy issues and proactively shape Leahy vetting for the future, DoD and DoS officials in Washington spend much of their energy managing the assembly line and responding to problematic cases against tight deadlines.

Time Lines for Vetting

We found few quantifiable data on how long the Leahy-vetting process actually takes from the submission of information until the embassy receives the determination made in Washington. The data we reviewed from INVEST accounted for only part of the process. Our interviewees cited varying lengths of time for seemingly similar requests. Most embassy interviewees reported that vetting time lines were not a significant issue or major cause of event cancellations, but some encountered significant delays and bottlenecks. When delays did occur, common sources included

- *Partner-nation delays.* Information requiring clarification or completion often includes rank, position, and date of birth.
- *Embassy delays.* Delays may result from late or incomplete submissions from embassy staff, competing tasks receiving greater priority than Leahy vetting, periods with high volumes of vetting requests, or technical issues with INVEST or embassy computers. Researching and adjudicating derogatory information also caused delays.
- *Delays at DoS headquarters.* Such delays were usually due to high volume and (for regional desk officers) competing priorities, but some interviewees expressed concern that DoS might delay discussions on politically contentious cases, resulting in last-minute announcements of decisions.

Clarity of Scope for Vetting

While our analysis showed that the guidance on what programs and activity types are subject to Leahy vetting was relatively clear, our interviews indicated that the challenge lies in translating this guidance into action. Interviewees cited difficulties in determining which programs and events required vetting, in part because of uncertainties about whether activities met the definitions of "training or other assistance." Embassy personnel reported three primary approaches to determining whether vetting was needed: deferring to program owners; using a rule of thumb, such as vetting military but not civilian personnel; or vetting everything, regardless of funding source.

Information Used for Vetting

Per DoS guidance, information from the INVEST database is mandated for use in vetting. Embassies are also directed to use other reliable and credible sources of information that are available, including embassy files; embassy Regional Security Office records; the Consular Lookout and Support system; the records of law-enforcement agencies and DoD offices at post; and outreach to human rights organizations, host-government officials, and media contacts.

Determining which other sources of information are credible is left to individual vetters. Interviewees expressed concern that DoS vetters taking questionable allegations at face value could taint whole organizations or several units, even if only select individuals had perpetrated the violation. In some instances, derogatory information, such as arrests for driving under the influence or domestic violence, might not involve gross human rights violations but could still adversely affect a unit or candidate's chances of being approved for training. In such cases, although the Leahy vetting process is the vehicle for vetting the individual, individuals are not approved for training for policy reasons rather than because the Leahy law explicitly forbids approval. This distinction between legal and policy-driven choices is sometimes lost on stakeholders.

DoD and embassy-level stakeholders often find case deliberations and determinations to be insufficiently inclusive. Decisionmaking about some cases at DoS headquarters may suffer from inadequate dialogue, perhaps due to a combination of deadline pressures, limited governance structures, and competing demands on staff time. The DoS decisionmaking process is not sufficiently transparent; DoS headquarters does not always adequately explain nonapprovals, resulting in significant frustration among both U.S. and partner-nation officials.

Embassies must sometimes deal with questionable information. At one embassy, an estimated 25 percent of data received from the partner nation required further investigation. This could include errors in basic information, such as an individual's name and date and place of birth. Best practices interviewees reported using to overcome these challenges included providing detailed guidance, researching the partner nation's military structure, and creating forms for the partner military to complete.

Adequacy of Training and Staff Resources

We identified few Leahy vetting officials who had previous experience or received formal training to prepare them for their responsibilities. Many interviewees who had received formal training considered it to be inadequate. Most interviewees reported staffing levels to handle Leahy vetting were adequate, in contrast to earlier research findings, although few embassies had staff working full time on Leahy vetting, which some reported problematic in times of high volume. Workloads were also considered to be high for those at DoS and DoD who oversaw the Leahy vetting process. With only a couple of exceptions, training and staffing at combatant commands (CCMDs) was not sufficient to enable their staffs to play a proactive role supporting DoD efforts to implement Leahy vetting and remediation and to integrate human rights considerations into security cooperation more generally.

Partner Relationships

In addition to problems with missing or unreliable information, embassy interviewees reported difficulty in obtaining information from partner nations. Embassy interviewees highlighted frustration at the lack of available organizational information from the partner nation.

Cancellation of training or denied participation in training (usually due to a suspension or rejection in the vetting process), particularly without a comprehensive explanation, can also be a sensitive issue with partner nations. Nevertheless, U.S. staff members being able to explain evidence of derogatory information to partners can resolve tensions in the relationship. Some interviewees reported this could also lead to stronger dialogue on human rights issues and reinforce bilateral engagement.

Key Findings and Recommendations

Some of the challenges of Leahy vetting might appear to be purely bureaucratic, such as work-arounds leading to unintended consequences and outdated technology complicating communication between officials in various parts of the U.S. government. But when the gears do not move smoothly, the machine does not function—and, in some instances, the result is a suboptimal outcome for U.S. policy goals on human rights. A fundamental purpose of Leahy implementation, after all, is to improve the human rights records of recipients of U.S. security assistance. The findings and recommendations presented in this report focus on helping DoD improve its capability to efficiently and effectively implement the Leahy laws. Chapter Three describes all our findings and recommendations, but here we summarize a few key findings and recommendations, with the main takeaways in bold.

Overall Findings

Our research found the Leahy-vetting requirements are generally not a roadblock to security cooperation, but its oversight is challenged by **inadequate governance structures**.

Process

The process does appear to be relatively effective at identifying human rights violators. Nevertheless, it **could be made more transparent to DoD stakeholders**. Much of the confusion regarding the process stems from the system's complexity—and from the lack of clear, transparent, consistent communication among all DoD and DoS stakeholders. Better communication through the use of working groups, better documentation of deliberations, and informal guidance should help increase transparency of the process.

There appear to be some challenges using the INVEST system to support policy analysis. For example, it is difficult for policymakers in Washington to analyze how many training events are executed, canceled, or postponed as a result of vetting decisions. Staff would have to gather and compile such data from individual embassies to perform this type of analysis at a macro level. Likewise, although INVEST uses 26 drop-down DoS and DoD funding categories, it has no Title

10 (DoD) vs. Title 22 (DoS) sorting or aggregating function, which makes it difficult for policymakers in Washington to separate DoD cases from DoS cases for purposes of analyzing implementation of the DoD Leahy law.

Remediation for a tainted unit requires leadership commitment and an iterative dialogue between Washington and the field. While some stakeholders argue that the remediation process is too cumbersome, some best practices now exist, and there may be opportunities to use informal guidance to help others start the process.

Time Lines

Few reported problems with process time lines, and those who did used several practices to overcome process challenges. Some best practices exist, while other practices can lead to their own problems. In particular, certain practices may create intense deadline pressures, making it harder to get ahead of an issue, and this may lead vetters to abandon proposed units or individuals that could be brought to resolution with further discussion.

Training

Improving training may improve implementation significantly. DoS and DoD training differs, and neither appears to focus sufficiently on managing the vetting process.

Overall Recommendations

Our research points to two overall recommendations. First, **four strategic working groups**—Process, Case Determination, Training and Staffing, and Partner Relationships—may help improve the Leahy vetting process and DoD's capacity to implement the Leahy law more generally. These working groups would replace and expand upon the current Incident Review Team structure and include representatives of DoS and DoD. National Security Council staff could also be empowered to participate directly in these working groups to help resolve differences and increase visibility on the issues. They would meet regularly to discuss ways to improve implementation and could report regularly—perhaps quarterly—to the Under Secretary of State for Civilian Security, Democracy, and Human Rights and the Under Secretary of

Defense for Policy. Second, for embassies with less than a 95-percent approval rating for Leahy vetting cases, **sub–working groups** may help in better preparing and informing stakeholders, leading to fewer misunderstandings and clearer outcomes.

Process

Our research points to several recommendations for process improvements:

- While complete standardization would be counterproductive, **partially standardizing all embassy standard operating procedures** through the use of template language could help make understanding of the Leahy process among stakeholders more consistent and comprehensive worldwide.
- Requiring vetters to use INVEST to **document,** in a reasonably automated fashion, the **deliberations** and decisions during each step of the process would increase transparency and trust.
- We recommend that DoS provide a way for more DoD stakeholders to access INVEST more easily.
- DoS and DoD should work together to improve INVEST's ability to support high-level analysis of the impact of case determinations on training events, as well as analysis of Title 10 cases and events in aggregate.
- The Process Working Group should hold a series of small **remediation workshops** with a range of U.S. government stakeholders to discuss the goals, costs, benefits, and risks of remediation in a strategic context. Supplementing Leahy remediation guidance with information-sharing mechanisms, such as best practices workshops and informal lists of **frequently asked questions** may improve the ability of stakeholders to pursue the remediation of tainted units and thereby broaden the influence of both the Leahy laws and security assistance. Efforts to supplement formal guidance with additional means of sharing information would improve understanding of the process and help demystify it.
- Developing a database to track cases in which individuals and units are approved for assistance but for whom derogatory infor-

mation is then revealed about past or subsequent acts could help enhance transparency and trust in the system.

Time Lines

Adding a five-day "second review" step to the end of the vetting time line for DoD Leahy law cases would allow the Case Determination Working Group to conduct additional research and discuss cases with what could be called "preliminary suspensions or cancellations." This will require vetters to submit cases slightly earlier than the current guidance directs, thus easing the pressures that sometimes erupt and allowing more time for open deliberation. After this new process step has been established and assessed, DoS and DoD could set a goal to reduce suspensions and cancellations, perhaps by a significant percentage, since the new process should make vetting more effective and with clearer outcomes.

Scope

Two steps may help clarify the scope of Leahy vetting requirements. OSD should update its formal guidance and supplement it with **informal guidance** that helps address real-world questions and scenarios to illustrate how vetters implement the guidance. For example, guidance could discuss in plain language how the line between activities that do and do not require vetting can be blurry, and steps security cooperation planners and vetting implementers can take to clarify their intent. DoD and DoS can also use the Case Determination Working Group to more transparently and inclusively deliberate over what information is determined to be credible and what is not.

Information Used

While most cases encounter no allegations of derogatory information, those that do can create significant dilemmas. Interviewees often felt they had little voice in final determinations on information credibility and perceived the process to be opaque and the determinations to be inconsistent. The Case Determination Working Group could be used to improve collaboration on determining information credibility. It could also develop a method to **document** these **deliberations** and thereby provide a source of information to benefit future discussions.

While there is an existing mechanism in place to convene and discuss Leahy vetting-related issues—the Incident Review Team process—our conversations with embassy, CCMD, DoS, and OSD officials suggest this process has proven inadequate. Because effective case determinations are central to effective Leahy implementation, greater collaboration and transparency in determining the credibility of derogatory information would likely help prevent or resolve many other Leahy vetting challenges. Therefore, we recommend replacing the existing Incident Review Team process with the Case Determination Working Group, which would be embedded in the overall governance structure we describe in Chapter Three.

Training

Most interviewees had no prior experience or formal training before taking on Leahy-vetting responsibilities, and most of those who had received training considered it inadequate. There were differences between DoS and DoD training, and in neither case did there seem to be a sufficient focus on managing the vetting process itself. There appeared to be a need for more training on the vetting process training and, more broadly, on security cooperation processes and human rights in general. While we found examples of innovative approaches to informal training, e.g., tips-of-the-week and cheat sheets, DoS and DoD made little effort to facilitate the sharing or institutionalization of these best practices. Staff dedicated to human-rights issues at two CCMDs did enable a more strategic, proactive approach to supporting Leahy-law implementation and promotion of human rights, whereas other CCMD staffs took a more hands-off, legalistic approach. In order for implementation of the Leahy laws to be strategically managed and well integrated with security assistance planning, the CCMDs should play a proactive role. We first recommend that the Training Working Group assess and **document the formal training requirements** for various participants in the Leahy-vetting process. This should include identifying categories of staff and the training that each requires. Second, the working group should create an **online annotated briefing** to supplement formal training. This could include a more broadly ranging section on frequently asked questions, regularly updated based on real-world questions posed by stakeholders, with links to working-group coordinators.

Partner Relationships

Finally, the Partner Relationships Working Group should hold a **series of small workshops** to better understand the challenges and best practices associated with engaging partners in Leahy vetting and human rights discussions. The group could discuss and document best practices with engaging partners and, ultimately, develop guidance for communicating with partners.

Acknowledgments

We greatly appreciate the assistance provided by our sponsor, Deputy Assistant Secretary of Defense for Stability and Humanitarian Affairs Anne Witkowsky, and her director for International Humanitarian Policy, Mark Stamilio. Also in the Office of the Secretary of Defense, we would like to thank Robert Kravinsky, who helped shape the original parameters of the study, and Mark Swayne, Walter Earle, Trent Buatte, Leo Cruz, and Lindsay Rodman, who supported the effort through its completion. We are also grateful to their Office of the Secretary of Defense and Joint Staff colleagues, who provided important insights throughout our research.

We also recognize the invaluable contributions of those leaders and experts we interviewed from the Department of State (DoS), as well as from several DoD combatant commands and U.S. embassies. We could not have completed our research without the generous support of officials from DoS Bureau of Democracy, Human Rights, and Labor, particularly Deputy Assistant Secretary of State Dafna Rand and her team. Officials from seven other DoS bureaus also provided important insights, as did DoD and DoS officials from 16 embassies and four combatant commands.

Thank you to our reviewers, James Schear and Larry Hanauer, who improved our draft report tremendously. Thank you to our editor, Phyllis Gilmore, and our administrative support staff. We appreciate the efforts of our RAND colleague, Steve Watts, who helped us shape the original research design and get the project off to a strong start.

Finally, we especially thank our communications analyst, Clifford Grammich, who greatly improved the quality of our report.

CHAPTER ONE

Introduction

Purpose

Protection of human rights is an essential American value—one enshrined directly in the Constitution and increasingly extended to foreign policy. Congress has made efforts to extend human rights and accountability considerations to relationships with U.S. foreign security partners. Among these efforts are two pieces of legislation collectively known as the *Leahy laws* after their author, Sen. Patrick Leahy (D-Vt.).[1] These prohibit the U.S. government from providing assistance or training to members or units of any nation's security forces that have perpetrated gross violations of human rights (GVHRs) with impunity.[2] The process for examining units and individuals for possible human rights violations is commonly referred to as *Leahy vetting*, an effort in which both the Department of Defense (DoD) and the Department of State (DoS) are key stakeholders.

---

[1] There are two pieces of legislation, but they have been revised over time, resulting in the impression that there are many Leahy laws.

[2] This formulation is a simplification of several overlapping pieces of legislation, most notably the Foreign Operations, Export Financing, and Related Programs Appropriations Act, 1998, PL 105-118, November 26, 1997; §8057 of the Department of Defense Appropriations Act, 2014 (in Consolidated Appropriations Act, 2014, PL 113-76, January 17, 2014); §620M, "Limitation on Assistance to Security Forces," in the Foreign Assistance Act of 1961, as amended through PL 114–195, enacted July 20, 2016; and §8058 in the Department of Defense Appropriations Act for FY 2012 (in Consolidated Appropriations Act, 2012, PL 112-74, December 23, 2011).

These two long-standing human rights provisions are also sometimes referred to as the *Leahy amendments* or as the *State Leahy law* and the *DoD Leahy law*. The first of these is Section 620M of the Foreign Assistance Act of 1961, as amended in 1998 (Public Law 87-195, 22 U.S.C. 2378d), which prohibits the DoS from furnishing assistance under the Foreign Assistance Act and the Arms Export Control Act to any foreign security force unit if the Secretary of State has credible information that the unit has committed a GVHR. The second is a recurring provision of the National Defense Authorization Act, first inserted to the act for fiscal year (FY) 2015 (Public Law 113-291, 10 USC 2249e), which prohibits the use of DoD funds to support any training program, later expanded to include equipment and other assistance, for members of a unit of a foreign security force if the Secretary of Defense (SECDEF) has credible information that the unit has committed a GVHR.

Leahy vetting is undertaken for a mix of programs that fall under Titles 10 and 22 of the U.S. Code (USC). Title 22 directs U.S. foreign assistance and falls under DoS purview; Title 10 directs the armed forces and is managed by DoD. However, both authorities provide the framework the U.S. government uses to legally share information with, train and equip, exercise with, and educate foreign security forces. As a result, security cooperation activities involve both DoS and DoD, which are jointly responsible for handling the U.S. government's overall relationship with partner militaries.

DoD officials recognize that the U.S. military is an institutional beneficiary of the Leahy laws. Before their enactment, human rights considerations in conducting security cooperation activities with partner nations were often ad hoc, subject to the ups and downs of congressional mood and unrelated geopolitical swings. Leahy vetting provides a framework for assessing the human rights component of security cooperation decisions. As a SECDEF memo of 2014 notes, "U.S. Forces' engagements with foreign security forces reflect U.S. values. The ethical and accountable behavior of our partner nation's security forces is critical to our long-term success."[3] Security cooperation efforts provide an opportunity to socialize these values with partner nations, and the Leahy vetting process often acts as an effective tool to improve dialogue and practice on human rights.

While the leadership of DoD and DoS unequivocally accept both the rationale and the utility of Leahy vetting, this outlook does not always filter down through every layer of these institutions. It is not uncommon to find DoD and DoS personnel who regard Leahy vetting as an impediment to security engagement with partner nations or an unwelcome bureaucratic burden.

Some objections about Leahy vetting may reflect a state of affairs long since past, largely addressed by revisions to the Leahy laws and further guidance from DoS and DoD, while others remain valid. Some concerns center around the general process and policies, while others are more specific, e.g., long time lines, lack of clarity about when Leahy vetting is required, questionable information used in vetting, inadequate training, and poor guidance for managing partner relationships. As discussed later, these concerns helped shape the questions that guided our research. Leahy vetting was always intended to be a continually improving process, and this report aims to provide insights and recommendations to help in that effort.

This report examines Leahy vetting from a process standpoint to help DoD improve its role in the existing system and build further capacity to implement the DoD Leahy law effectively, with transparency and accountability for results. The multistage Leahy process consists of submitting identification information on individuals and units and vetting through an online tracking system at U.S. embassies abroad before further vetting and status determination at DoS headquarters in Washington, D.C.

---

[3]   Office of the Secretary of Defense (OSD), guidance memo, August 18, 2014, Not available to the general public.

Research Questions

Since the enactment of the first DoD Leahy law in 1998, DoD has relied on the DoS to vet security assistance. DoS established the International Vetting and Security Tracking (INVEST) system, which replaced the old cable-based process in 2010, to vet proposed recipients of DoD training; since 2014, this review has also included recipients of equipment and other assistance.[4] As we discuss in Chapter Two, although DoS manages that system, DoD determines candidates for training, proposes transfers of equipment, and generally serves as the primary liaison between the U.S. government and the command structure of a partner nation's military forces. This report examines the Leahy process writ large (rather than focusing solely on DoD's role in it) to better portray where the vetting procedure works well, where DoD could benefit from targeted improvements, and what best practices DoD could implement more broadly. Whether DoS or DoD or both handle the specific parts of the process, it is in DoD's interest to have a clear picture of how the process works—and where the department must overcome challenges. We developed several key research questions, based on initial discussions with the sponsor and other stakeholders:

- What procedural and policy challenges does Leahy vetting have?
- What are the time lines for vetting?
- How clear is the scope for vetting; that is, is it clear which programs and activities require vetting and which do not?
- What information is used for vetting and how is its credibility determined?
- Are current training and staffing resources adequate?
- What issues does Leahy vetting raise for partner relationships?

---

[4] DoD, "Report for Fiscal Year 2014 in Response to Section 1204(b) of the Carl Levin and Howard P. 'Buck' McKeon National Defense Authorization Act for Fiscal Year 2015, P.L. 113-291," March 31, 2015, p. 2.

Methodology

We organized our research into three phases. In Phase One, we developed a baseline understanding of DoD's current role in the Leahy vetting process, possible challenges, and common perceptions of the process. We reviewed existing documents and conducted preliminary interviews with key stakeholders in Washington and at DoD's combatant commands (CCMDs). In Phase Two, we interviewed both DoD and DoS Leahy vetting practitioners, reviewed embassy standard operating procedures (SOPs), and analyzed INVEST data to identify areas for improvement and to derive current best practices. In Phase Three, we identified continuing challenges and developed options for DoD to improve its capacity to implement the Leahy law.

Phases of the Research
Phase One: Understanding DoD's Role in Leahy Vetting, Possible Challenges, and Common Perceptions
To develop our baseline understanding, we analyzed current documents that provide guidance to DoS and DoD implementers, reviewed the existing body of literature on Leahy vetting, and conducted preliminary interviews with key stakeholders in Washington and at the CCMDs.

As part of this background and analysis of prior reports, we examined the various changes to Leahy laws since 1998. We also analyzed the guidance, definitions, and steps related to the Leahy vetting process contained in the DoS compliance guide, DoD's latest guidance on Leahy vetting implementation, and the February 2015 joint DoS-DoD policy document on remediation and resumption of assistance.[5] We reviewed DoD's annual reports to Congress for FYs 2014 and 2015 required by Public Law 113-291 and all publicly available CRS and GAO reports

---

[5] DoS, "Compliance with the State and DoD Leahy Laws: A Guide to Vetting Policy & Process," Washington, D.C., September 2012; OSD, 2014; DoD and DoS, "The Joint Department of Defense and DoS Policy on Remediation and the Resumption of Assistance Under the Leahy Laws," February 2015.

on Leahy vetting.[6] We also reviewed DoS Inspector General reports on problems with Leahy-vetting implementation at specific embassies and the chapter on human rights contained in the Defense Institute of Security Assistance Management's (DISAM's) Green Book.[7] We reviewed nongovernmental organization (NGO) reports and academic articles.[8] Finally, we searched ISCS's website, Google Scholar, and the Defense Technical Information Center for gray literature—for hard-to-find studies and reports not published commercially—on the implementation of Leahy vetting written by current or previous practitioners.

Following the key document review and analysis of existing studies on Leahy vetting, a series of face-to-face interviews with key stakeholders at OSD-Policy and DoS DRL helped us identify perceived obstacles to effective and efficient Leahy law implementation.

Phase One also informed the development of the interview protocols that were used in the practitioner interviews during Phase Two.

Phase Two: Selection of Focus Countries and Collection of Empirical Evidence

Phase Two involved selection of the 20 focus countries and collection of empirical evidence from

---

[6] DoD, 2015; DoD, "Report for Fiscal Year 2015 in response to Section1204(b) of the Carl Levin and Howard P. 'Buck' McKeon National Defense Authorization Act for Fiscal Year 2015," P.L. 113-291, March 31, 2016; Nina M. Serafino, June S. Beittel, Lauren Ploch Blanchard, and Liana Rosen, *"Leahy Law" Human Rights Provisions and Security Assistance: Issue Overview*, Washington, D.C.: Congressional Research Service, R43361, January 29, 2014; GAO, "Human Rights: Additional Guidance, Monitoring, and Training Could Improve Implementation of the Leahy Laws," Washington, D.C., GAO-13-866, September 2013; GAO, "Security Assistance: U.S. Government Should Strengthen End-Use Monitoring and Human Rights Vetting for Egypt," Washington, D.C., GAO-16-435, April 2016.

[7] Defense Institute of Security Assistance Management, *DISAM's Online Green Book: The Management of Security Assistance*, 2007–2008. On July 1, 2016, DISAM became the Institute of Security Cooperation Studies (ISCS).

[8] See, for example, Kayla Ruble, "Nigerian President Blames US Human Rights Law for 'Aiding and Abetting' Boko Haram," Vice News website, July 23, 2015; David Womack, "Human Rights Vetting: The Process and Lessons Learned," *ISCS Journal*, July 2007; see also Sara Egozi, "Aid Is Key to Reform Local Forces on Rights, Leahy Says," Washington, D.C.: United States Institute of Peace, February 12, 2016.

- interviews with practitioners who implement the Leahy vetting process at embassies in the focus countries
- a review and analysis of the Leahy vetting SOPs used at embassies in the focus countries
- interviews with Leahy vetting points of contact at the CCMDs
- interviews or discussions with Leahy vetters at DoS headquarters
- interviews or discussions with stakeholders at DoS regional bureaus, OSD, and the Joint Staff
- review and analysis of aggregated data from DoS's INVEST database.

Selection of Focus Countries

We selected our focus countries from the 156 countries that receive military and police aid from the United States, considering whether each country receives fast-track aid, the amount of military and police aid it receives, and its assigned CCMD.

We first sorted the 156 countries by type of Leahy process used at the embassy: fast-track or traditional. If DoS has determined that a country does not have a history of human rights abuse, vetting is completed at the embassy; this is referred to as *fast-track* vetting. In other cases, the traditional Leahy vetting process applies, in which cases are vetted both at post and in Washington, with the final determination being in made in Washington.[9]

We then grouped countries by the amount of U.S. military and police aid they received in 2014, using publicly available data from the Center for International Policy's Security Assistance Monitor website.[10] We separated countries into three groups: those that received what we considered a relatively large amount of aid (more than $20 million in

---

[9] See U.S. Department of State, "Leahy Vetting: Law, Policy, Process," briefing slides, Washington, D.C., April 15, 2013.

[10] We chose the Center for International Policy's Security Assistance Monitor website because it aggregates U.S. foreign assistance by country under the category "Military and Police Aid," while the U.S. government's foreign assistance website (U.S. Government, Foreign Assistance website, beta, undated) and USAID's Greenbook (USAID, "The Greenbook," website, April 29, 2013) do not.

FY 2014), a moderate amount of aid (from $1 million to $20 million in FY 2014), and a low amount of aid (less than $1 million in FY 2014).

Finally, we sorted countries according to geographic CCMDs (U.S. Africa Command, U.S. European Command, U.S. Central Command, U.S. Pacific Command, U.S. Southern Command [USSOUTHCOM], and U.S. Northern Command [USNORTHCOM]). Tables 1.1–1.6 depict the distribution of the 156 countries after this three-stage sorting process.[11]

We eliminated from further consideration the 71 countries that received less than $1 million in military and police aid in FY 2014, reasoning that such a low volume of aid likely resulted in a low number of Leahy-vetting cases. From the remaining 85 countries, we selected 20 focus countries that could represent each type of vetting process and each level of aid within each CCMD. We also relied on our review of prior studies and consultations with our sponsor to select focus countries. Table 1.7 shows the distribution of our 20 focus countries by Leahy process, amount of aid, and geographic CCMD. We sought to select multiple countries perceived as having particularly effective processes, multiple countries that had been categorized by DoS as having human rights concerns, and multiple countries that had been perceived as Leahy success stories (e.g., countries in which positive change within the partner nation government on human rights was attributed to Leahy vetting).

Collection of Interview Data

We conducted face-to-face and phone interviews with over 75 officials from eight DoS bureaus, 17 U.S. embassies, four CCMDs, and two DoD agencies. Officials included military officers, DoD civilians, Foreign Service officers, locally employed staff, eligible family members, and U.S. government contractors. We took detailed notes of each interview session, transcribing these notes for further review by a second researcher. For the DoS and CCMD interviews, we extracted passages

---

[11] In all the tables in this chapter, *traditional* refers to vetting at both the embassy and DoS headquarters, while *fast track* refers to vetting only at embassy, per DoS cable (09 STATE 87762). For funding, *large* is more than $20 million per year; *moderate* is more than $1 million but less than $20 million per year; and *low* is less than $1 million per year.

Table 1.1
Countries Receiving U.S. Military and Police Aid in FY 2014:
Africa Command

Leahy Process	Amount of Military and Police Aid	Number of Countries	Countries
Traditional	Large	6	Kenya, Mali, Niger, Somalia, South Sudan, Tunisia
	Moderate	21	Algeria, Angola, Burkina Faso, Burundi, Central African Republic, Democratic Republic of the Congo, Djibouti, Ethiopia, Ghana, Liberia, Libya, Mauritania, Morocco, Mozambique, Nigeria, Rwanda, Sengal, South Africa, Tanzania, Uganda, Zimbabwe
	Low	19	Benin, Botswana, Cameroon, Cape Verde, Chad, Comoros, Cote d'Ivoire, Gabon, Guinea, Lesotho, Malawi, Namibia, Republic of the Congo, São Tomé and Príncipe, Sierra Leone, Swaziland, Gambia, Togo, Zambia
Fast track	Large	0	
	Moderate	0	
	Low	2	Mauritius, Seychelles

SOURCE: Center for International Policy, undated.

Table 1.2
Countries Receiving U.S. Military and Police Aid in FY 2014:
European Command

Leahy Process	Amount of Military and Police Aid	Number of Countries	Countries
Traditional	Large	4	Georgia, Israel, Russia, Ukraine
	Moderate	9	Albania, Armenia, Azerbaijan, Bosnia, Kosovo, Moldova, Montenegro, Serbia, Turkey
	Low	1	Belarus
Fast track	Large	2	Bulgaria, Romania
	Moderate	9	Croatia, Czech, Estonia, Hungary, Latvia, Lithuania, Macedonia, Poland, Slovenia
	Low	11	Austria, Finland, Germany, Greece, Ireland, Malta, Portugal, Slovakia, Slovenia, Sweden, Switzerland

SOURCE: Center for International Policy, undated.

Table 1.3
Countries Receiving U.S. Military and Police Aid in FY 2014:
Central Command

Leahy Process	Amount of Military and Police Aid	Number of Countries	Countries
Traditional	Large	13	Afghanistan, Egypt, Iraq, Jordan, Lebanon, Kazakhstan, Kyrgyzstan, Pakistan, Palestine, Syria, Tajikistan, Uzbekistan, Yemen
	Moderate	2	Bahrain, Oman
	Low	4	Qatar, Saudi Arabia, Turkmenistan, United Arab Emirates
Fast track	Large	0	
	Moderate	0	
	Low	0	

SOURCE: Center for International Policy, undated.

Table 1.4
Countries Receiving U.S. Military and Police Aid in FY 2014:
Pacific Command

Leahy Process	Amount of Military and Police Aid	Number of Countries	Countries
Traditional	Large	2	Indonesia, Philippines
	Moderate	11	Bangladesh, Burma, Cambodia, India, Loas, Maldives, Malaysia, Nepal, Sri Lankia, Thailand, Vietnam
	Low	11	Bhutan, Brunei, China, Fiji, Hong Kong, Niue, Papua New Guinea, Samoa, Singapore
Fast track	Large	0	
	Moderate	1	Mongolia
	Low	7	Kiribati, Marshall Islands, Micronesia, Palua, South Korea, Tuvalu, Vanuatu

SOURCE: Center for International Policy, undated.

related to best practices and implementation challenges. We coded these extracted passages by topic to facilitate analysis in Phase Three. For the country team interviews, we compiled a database on 86 data

Table 1.5
Countries Receiving U.S. Military and Police Aid in FY 2014:
Southern Command

Leahy Process	Amount of Military and Police Aid	Number of Countries	Countries
Traditional	Large	2	Colombia, Peru
	Moderate	10	Brazil, Dominican Republic, Ecuador, El Salvador, Guatemala-, Haiti, Honduras, Nicaragua, Panama, Uruguay
	Low	7	Argentina, Bolivia, Guyana, Jamaica, Paraguay, Suriname, Venezuela
Fast track	Large	0	
	Moderate	2	Chile, Costa Rica
	Low	8	Antigua and Barbuda, Barbados, Dominica, Grenada, St Kitts and Nevis, St Vincent and the Grenadines, Trinidad and Tobago, Uruguay

SOURCE: Center for International Policy, undated.

Table 1.6
Countries Receiving U.S. Military and Police Aid in FY 2014:
Northern Command

Leahy Process	Amount of Military and Police Aid	Number of Countries	Countries
Traditional	Large	1	Mexico
	Moderate	0	
	Low	0	
Fast track	Large	0	
	Moderate	0	
	Low	1	Bahamas

SOURCE: Center for International Policy, undated.

points, with emphasis on 34 of the most important, highest-priority questions. We analyzed this database in Phase Three.

Table 1.7
Distribution of the 20 Focus Countries by Leahy-Vetting Process, Amount
of Aid, and Geographic Combatant Command

Leahy Process	Amount of Military and Police Aid	Number of Focus Countries, by Combatant Command					
		Africa	European	Central	Pacific	Southern	Northern
Traditional	Large	2	1	2	2	1	1
	Moderate	3	1	1	1	2	0
	Low	0	0	0	0	0	0
Fast track	Large	0	0	0	0	0	0
	Moderate	0	1	0	1	1	0
	Low	0	0	0	0	0	0

Collection of Leahy-Vetting SOP Data

We also reviewed Leahy-vetting SOPs from 16 of our 20 focus countries. We compiled a database on 36 data points for analysis in Phase Three.

Collection of INVEST data

We met with staff of the DoS DRL office that manages the INVEST database. DRL staff members familiarized the team with several aggregated reports that INVEST generates. We were not able to access raw INVEST data, but DRL staff provided us with summary data that included the numbers of Leahy cases that were submitted, approved, suspended, rejected, and canceled within each of DoS's six regional bureaus (Africa, East Asia and the Pacific, Europe and Eurasia, Near Eastern Affairs, South and Central Asia, and Western Hemisphere) from 2010 through April 7, 2016. Data from FY 2010 and FY 2016 are not complete.

Phase Three: Analyzing the Empirical Evidence and Development of Findings

In Phase Three, we analyzed the compiled empirical evidence and identified trends and detailed examples of best practices and problem areas relating to our six research questions. Chapter Three details this analysis and offers findings for each of the six questions.

Limitations of This Research

Our research had several limitations. First, our sponsor tasked us with a process-focused analysis of Leahy vetting. While we recognize the importance of understanding the policy goals behind the Leahy laws, we do not provide an analysis of how or how well the Leahy laws help encourage countries to improve their human rights standards and performance.

Second, our findings may not be generalizable to all aspects of Leahy vetting. Some may be relevant only at the headquarters level, others at the embassy level. Some may be relevant only to DoD. Finally, because each embassy has its own internal vetting practices, some of our results may reflect a one-size-fits-one approach.

Third, the best practices and challenges we identified do not represent all possible best practices and challenges. Rather, they reflect those we were able to describe through firsthand accounts and primary documents from DoD and DoS headquarters and embassies at the 20 countries on which we focused.

Fourth, while we tried to interview a broad array of stakeholders, limited access to participants and documents may have skewed the results of this research toward particular stakeholder equities.

The remainder of this chapter provides additional background on the Leahy laws and their implementation. In Chapter Two, we highlight some insights derived from our interviews relevant to each of our six research questions. In Chapter Three, we describe our most important findings and provide recommendations for how DoD and other stakeholders may wish to address them.

Background on the Leahy Vetting Process

The Leahy Laws

The Leahy laws comprise two separate pieces of legislation sponsored by Sen. Patrick Leahy (D-Vt.). First, the "State Leahy law"—Section 620M of the Foreign Assistance Act of 1961, as amended in 1998 (22 U.S.C. 2378d)—prohibits the furnishing of assistance under the Foreign Assistance Act and the Arms Export Control Act to any foreign security force unit if the Secretary of State has credible information that the unit has committed a GVHR. Second, the "DoD Leahy law," which existed as a recurring provision inserted into annual defense appropriation acts prior to the Carl Levin and Howard P. "Buck" McKeon National Defense Authorization Act for Fiscal Year 2015 (10 U.S.C. 2249e), prohibits the use of DoD funds to support any training program—a prohibition expanded in 2015 to include equipment and other assistance—for members of a unit of a foreign security force if SECDEF has credible information that the unit has committed a GVHR.

For the first decade and a half of the Leahy laws' existence, there was considerable confusion about what types of U.S. security assistance required vetting. Since the laws' inception in 1998, Congress has increasingly aligned the language of the DoS and DoD Leahy laws and instituted two recent changes that significantly expanded the requirement for vetting. In 2014, Congress expanded the DoD Leahy law and aligned it more closely with the DoS law by stating that the vetting requirement applied to "any training, equipment or other assistance."[12] While this helped define relevant cooperation, the perennial challenge for implementers of differentiating "assistance" from "cooperation" remains.

Under current law, the vetting requirement includes both the individual designated for training and the individual's unit.[13] In practice, units to be vetted are determined on a case-by-case basis. DoS has viewed the relevant unit as "the lowest organizational element of a security force capable of exercising command and discipline over its members."[14]

Guidance on Policy and Process

In its 2012 guide on compliance with the Leahy laws, DoS provides an overview of vetting policy and process, as well as references to supplement guidance and specific policy cables, such as the cable that identifies Fast Track countries and the cable that establishes the policy of vet-

---

[12] 10 USC 2249e.

[13] Consolidated Appropriations Act, 2014 (Division F, §7034(l), P.L. 113-76).

[14] Joint Staff, "Human Rights Verification for DOD-Funded Training of Foreign Personnel," policy message, DTG071300Z, June 2004.

ting being "good for one year."[15] The DoS guide includes extracts from the Foreign Affairs Manual which provides key definitions and examples for derogatory information (DI), GVHRs, and non–human rights violations that could disqualify a nominee from receiving training.

The DoS guide identifies eight steps in Leahy vetting and provides an overview of INVEST, the official system for vetting foreign security forces, put in place between 2010 and 2011.[16] The GAO succinctly summarizes the vetting process in a figure replicated in Figure 1.1.

DoD does not appear in this figure, despite the fact that DoD has important equities and involvement in implementing the Leahy laws

Figure 1.1
U.S. Human Rights Vetting Process

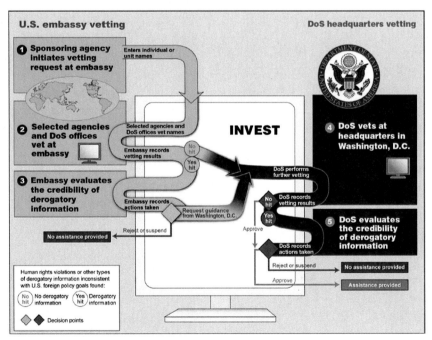

SOURCE: GAO, 2013.
RAND RR1737-1.1

---

[15] DoS, 2012.

[16] DoS, 2012.

(particularly the DoD Leahy laws). All DoD-funded vetting requests, however, originate at embassies with DoD officers assigned there—all of whom have access to INVEST. As we will discuss later, this perception of a limited role is at the heart of the challenges DoD stakeholders face in having the transparency and voice they need to execute their responsibilities in this system.

The DoS guide notes that a minimum of ten working days must be allotted for the vetting process in Washington. DoS advises embassies to plan adequate lead time for vetting at the embassy and in Washington to raise "the probability of successfully vetting candidates in time for their training or assistance."[17]

Lastly, the guide encourages country teams to develop written SOPs, which tailor department-level guidance to meet the particular needs and circumstances of their posts, as embassies vary in resources and the security forces of partner nations vary by history and demographics. Thus, the information used to vet at the embassy level may vary by country. DoS mandates that embassies use the INVEST Database and Document Library, which contains information from past vetting. It advises embassies to "use as many reliable and credible sources of information as are available," including embassy files, Regional Security Office records, the Consular Lookout and Support System, the records of the law enforcement agencies and DoD offices at post, and the Internet, as well as outreach to local Human Rights NGOs, government officials, and media contacts.[18] The DoS guide on vetting suggests tips for effective searches, such as using multiple variations of a name, trying different search terms, and conducting additional searches if DI is vague or unreliable.[19]

DoS officials said that the guide is currently undergoing revisions and that the new version will reflect the 2014 changes to the DoD Leahy law. The 2014 changes are now posted on the DoS intranet site, accessible to anyone with a DoS account. Changes are also noted in bulletins to INVEST users. DoS also posted updated guidance and

---

[17] DoS, 2012

[18] DoS, 2012.

[19] DoS, 2012.

informed vetters the day after the DoD guidance was promulgated in September 2014.

Latest DoD-Specific Policy and Guidance

In August 2014, SECDEF provided the services, Joint Staff, and CCMDs with implementation guidance on significant changes to the DoD Leahy law that appeared in Section 8057, DoD Appropriations Act, 2014 (Division C of Public Law 113-76).[20] SECDEF directed DoD to vet foreign security forces using INVEST and provided guidance on exemptions to the Leahy law (e.g., in disaster-relief operations) and a process for obtaining waivers in extraordinary circumstances. The memorandum also provided extensive definitions for what training, equipment, and other assistance is subject to the Leahy law. Finally, SECDEF attempted to clarify the scope of required vetting by identifying how the Leahy law affects DoD authorities and programs.[21] This guidance specifies that most programs require Leahy vetting but also identifies several programs that do not require vetting because they benefit the United States as much as or more than the partner countries. For some programs, the guidance is not definitive, and for others it directs the reader to "refer to the relevant statutory authorities."[22]

Remediation Policy and Guidance

A 2015 joint DoS-DoD policy document outlines standards for remediation and resumption of assistance.[23] Remediation is the process in which partner nations take corrective action regarding ineligible units tainted with GVHR in return for resumed aid and assistance. The policy document seeks to reconcile incongruities between the DoS and DoD Leahy laws that set different criteria determining when assistance can recommence and better align the DoS and DoD approaches to the laws.

---

[20] OSD, 2014. Previous DoD guidance came in Joint Staff, 2004.

[21] OSD, 2014.

[22] OSD, 2014

[23] DoD and DoS, 2015.

CHAPTER TWO

Vetting Challenges and Best Practices

Our task in our interviews was threefold: to analyze current implementation of Leahy law provisions and DoD's role in it, to evaluate best practices and challenges, and to recommend options for improvement in the six areas we identified for consideration. These six areas, which are based on initial discussions with stakeholders and structured to capture the widest possible range of challenges faced by the Leahy vetting program, are

- process and policy challenges, including common procedures and practices and use of the INVEST system
- time lines for vetting, including schedules, delays, and bottlenecks
- clarity of scope for vetting, including determining when vetting is required
- information used for vetting, including sources and types
- adequacy of training and other resources for vetting, including staffing allocation and preparation
- partner relationships, including maintenance of diplomatic and military relationships.

We review each of these areas in turn below. The information that follows is by no means intended to serve as a comprehensive review of our interviews or an endorsement of the points made. What follows, rather, are select insights that illustrate some of the many perspectives we collected from practitioners around the world. These insights, combined with those from our examination of existing research—as well as many other insights too voluminous to document in a report as concise as this one—helped inform the findings and recommendations provided in Chapter Three.

Process and Policy Challenges and Best Practices

DoD Process Ownership and Variation in Implementation Practices

One important process and policy challenge we identified in our research was the need to balance the efficiencies and synergies that come from using a single vetting process (maintained by DoS) to implement both the DoS and DoD Leahy laws with the need to ensure that DoD can execute its responsibilities for cases that fall under the DoD Leahy law. Our analysis of document and interview data made it clear that DoD needs to be a more equal partner in the vetting process, yet many DoD stakeholders, from embassies to CCMDs to the Pentagon, do not perceive DoD as having sufficient involvement in this process.

Another key challenge was inconsistent approaches to implementing Leahy at the embassy level. Both CRS and GAO reports have noted the lack of standardization in Leahy vetting practices and procedures implemented at posts.[1] Given the variety of circumstances at posts, it is DoS policy to delegate SOPs to suit each unique situation. Each embassy maintains its own SOP; there is no government-wide model SOP.[2] As a result, each post has adopted a different set of internal processes and practices for producing results within the broader Leahy vetting process. Of course, some tailoring is important, and DoS does provide standard building blocks to posts that are drafting SOPs. Nevertheless, a model SOP—based on a template identifying minimum information requirements—would be valuable for many implementers. It could also help institutionalize some of the procedures that were sometimes cited in our embassy interviews as best (or at least good) practices.

The four practices that follow illustrate ways that both DoD and DoS implementers can effectively execute their responsibilities at the

---

[1] Serafino et al., 2014; GAO, 2013.

[2] It should be noted that, although each SOP is unique to each post, they are reviewed by DoS headquarters.

embassy level, while also pointing to important themes, such as relationship-building, coordination mechanisms, and partner relationships, which we explore later in this chapter.

Develop an Internal Coordination Mechanism

Some of our embassy-level interviewees noted internal coordination mechanisms within their posts, such as a Leahy vetting working group or council. These working groups have multiple sections at a post and are convened in person or by email. An example of a Leahy vetting council provided to us includes the deputy chief of mission, the post's Leahy vetting coordinator, and relevant embassy section heads such as the political officer, consular officer, regional security officer, defense attaché, and security cooperation officer.[3] Working groups provide a platform for the interagency stakeholders involved in Leahy vetting to discuss difficult issues, such as DI hits or GVHR allegations, decisions to cancel or postpone training, and requests from partner countries.

Build Relationships with Sections at Post and Vetters at DoS Headquarters

Relationship building and management was a consistent theme throughout our interviews with DoS and DoD officials at post, CCMD staff members, and DoS headquarters employees. At posts, positive relations between the embassy sections and the Leahy vetting coordinator (often a political officer) streamlined the process, made for easier adjudication of issues, and often let to more successful vetting outcomes.[4] For example, a vetting coordinator noted that her close relationship with embassy staff involved in complex, technical activities helped her translate their jargon into a form that DoS headquarters would understand, increasing the successful vetting of these batches.[5] Holding good relationships with DoS headquarters vetters was also seen as critical to handling cases with potential DI, ensuring that vetting cases and batches are received in time for training events, and

---

3   Interview with U.S. official, April 2016.

4   Interviews with U.S. officials, March and May 2016.

5   Interview with U.S. official, May 2016.

pushing through short-fuse requests.[6] For the purposes of Leahy vetting, *cases* are single individuals or units identified to receive training, and *batches* are aggregations of cases.

Proactively Manage Vetting Requests

The process, from initial submission to final determination, is not automatic and requires active input, tracking, and following up on vetting requests at all stages. Our interviews found several proactive best practices for managing and streamlining vetting requests, including the following:

- the Leahy vetting coordinator or assistant sending weekly reminders of deadlines and updates on submitted vetting batches to sections
- vetting alternative candidates for training, so long as they are well qualified, in case the existing candidate is not approved (One interviewee noted that he kept a database of prevetted individuals that he could send to an event at any time, which was useful for short-fuse requests,although individuals should not be sent simply to fill an empty seat).[7]
- submitting multiple individuals and units for multiple events as single batches (Two embassies reported that they have pushed for unit vetting or packaging multiple training activities as a single vetting batch, rather than sending multiple individual vetting requests).[8]
- avoiding "best case scenarios," by building time into a vetting request to ensure deadlines are met or that there is ample time to investigate and clarify reported DI.

Streamline Processes to Obtain Partner Nation Information

Many interviewees noted that they had employed several strategies to streamline the process of obtaining information from their partner

---

[6]   Interviews with U.S. officials, March and April 2016.

[7]   Interview with U.S. official, March 2016.

[8]   Interviews with U.S. officials, March and May 2016.

countries. This includes creating standardized forms in English and other languages and setting hard-stop submission deadlines.

International Vetting and Security Tracking System

DoS uses INVEST to vet foreign security forces. Put in place between 2010 and 2011, INVEST is the official system for processing Leahy vetting for training.[9] The system is known to have significant limitations; for example, interviewees described it as "clunky," "like 1990s dial-up," and "just a gigantic spreadsheet."[10] Although our analysis found that some concerns about INVEST were justified, the creation of a database to record and track all cases in one location did bring considerable standardization and transparency to a process that had previously been far more variable and opaque. The database was being updated during our research, which should address some of the most serious technology-related complaints.

INVEST houses records of vetting for potential human rights abuses or other criminal activity by individuals and security force units. Under current law, the vetting requirement includes both the individual designated for training and the individual's unit.[11] DoS provided us aggregate INVEST reports. In Figures 2.1 and 2.2, we review what these indicate in terms of Leahy vetting outcomes, cases over time, and cases by region.

Figure 2.1 shows the vetting results for all training candidates from 2011 to 2015.[12] DoS has vetted more than 824,666 cases since 2011. DoD users noted that INVEST would be more valuable as a planning and management tool if they could use it to aggregate data on individuals and units in a way that facilitated analysis.

---

[9] Serafino et al., 2014.

[10] Interviews with U.S. officials, March and July 2016.

[11] Consolidated Appropriations Act, 2014 (Division F, §7034(l), P.L. 113-76)

[12] 2016 data are excluded as this report was written at the midpoint of the calendar year.

Figure 2.1
Vetting Action Outcomes Over Time

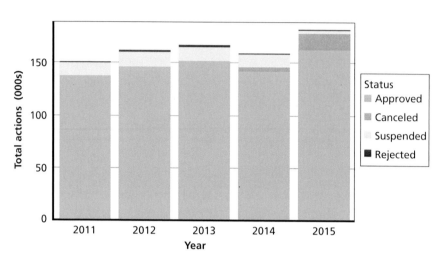

RAND RR1737-2.1

Total cases vary by region.[13] The western hemisphere is by far the largest region for Leahy vetting requests, generating the most cases of any region in each year of the data. Figure 2.2 shows the number of cases by region over time.

Vetting Outcomes in INVEST

INVEST indicates one of four possible outcomes for each case: approval, rejection, suspension, or cancellation. From 2011–2015, almost 90 percent of all cases were approved.

Figure 2.3 shows the total number of actions other than approval that DoS has taken. Rejection, which results in the withholding of training or assistance, is rare. In the dataset, the average rejection rate was 0.3 percent per year. This finding echoes other reports on INVEST data.[14] Cases are suspended when there is potential DI related to individuals or units and when DoS DRL and the relevant regional

---

[13] We were unable to analyze data by country because DoS is updating its database and country was not easily available.

[14] Emily Cadei, "Foreign Militaries, Domestic Tension," *CQ Weekly*, December 16, 2013.

Figure 2.2
INVEST Cases, by Region and Year

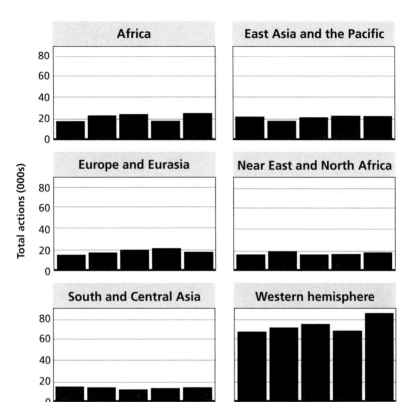

RAND RR1737-2.2

bureau—often without DoD input—cannot agree on whether the information is credible or warrants a rejection. Cases are canceled for administrative reasons, such as incomplete information that cannot be resolved in time for the individual to participate in a scheduled event.

As Figure 2.3 shows, the number of suspensions has decreased greatly since the introduction of the cancellation category in 2014. Prior to 2014, when there was no cancellation designation, the suspension decision could also be used for administrative reasons. For example, a vetter who had incomplete information and could not get sufficient information to complete the vetting in time would categorize it

Figure 2.3
INVEST Actions Other Than Approvals

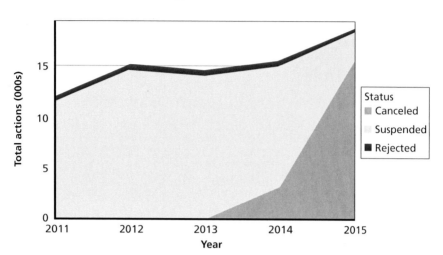

NOTE: The years along the x-axis represent the end point of each given year. Thus, the area between 2011 and 2012 represents the time between January and December of 2012, and so on.

RAND RR1737-2.3

as a suspension prior to 2014 but would categorize it as a cancellation today. Suspensions are now reserved "for cause" when there is not sufficient time or additional information to assess the accuracy of GVHR or other DI allegations.

As the data demonstrate, the introduction of the cancellation disposition led to a shift in designations from suspension to cancellation. This suggests that the majority of suspensions in prior years may have been related to administrative issues. For example, data entry problems may have caused a case to be suspended because INVEST designations are final. Another possibility is that operators may be using cancellations rather than suspensions for borderline cases because cancellations do not carry the same stigma, that of potential DI. Our interviews provided anecdotes supporting both possibilities. Figure 2.4 plots dispositions other than approval by region. The western hemisphere accounts for the largest number of rejections, which is not surprising given the volume of cases and history of GVHR by some countries.

Figure 2.4
INVEST Nonapprovals, by Type, Region, and Year

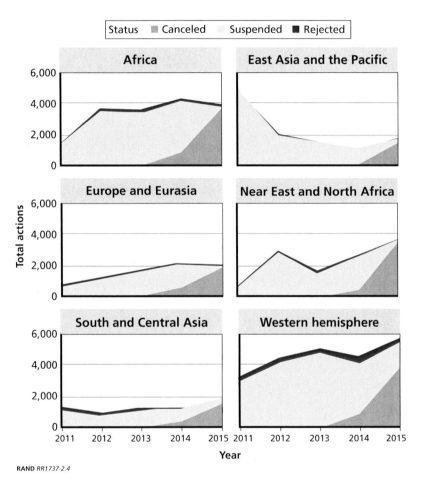

RAND *RR1737-2.4*

Figure 2.5 plots the same data as a percentage of all actions in a region. The nonapproval rate for the western hemisphere has been relatively low and steady in the past five years. South and Central Asia has seen an uptick in suspension rates as a percentage of total cases, while the percentages for the other regions generally follow their aggregate trends.

Cancellations increased sharply across all regions. Both posts and DoS headquarters are increasingly using the designation. A more in-

Figure 2.5
INVEST Nonapprovals as Percentage of All Actions, by Type, Region, and Year

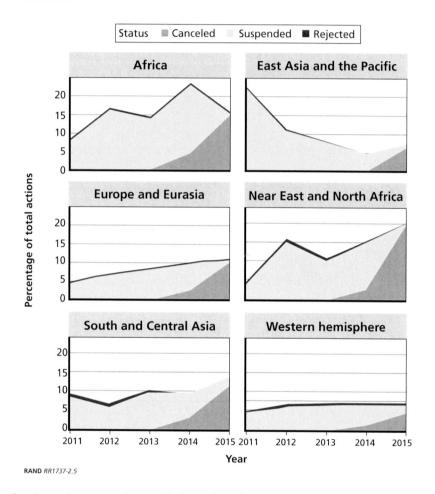

depth analysis may be needed to identify the primary driver of administrative problems and potential ways to reduce them.

We also examined the proportions of late cases from 2011–2015. A submission is late if it arrives after the 10-day "need-by" date for DoS headquarters or within ten days of the actual training. The need-by date may be more than ten days before training because DoS headquarters may request earlier submissions for cases that may take longer to process. Using data from DoS, we looked at the number of late sub-missions and the number of late violations from 2011–2015. Figure 2.6 shows the percentage of late submissions by year.

As shown in Figure 2.6, a sizeable minority of INVEST submissions are considered late by the time they reach DoS headquarters, ranging in 2015 from 10 percent for the western hemisphere to over 45 percent for Africa. These submissions are based on batches submitted within ten days of the beginning of assistance. Late submissions make vetting more difficult and can potentially lead to cancellations of events for administrative reasons if DoS headquarters is unable to process batches in time.

From earlier data, it is clear that DoS headquarters is able to turn around the vast majority of late cases, so trainings do not need to be canceled. Nonetheless, the current system has several problems. First, consistent lateness of submissions leads to a constant churn of cases and thus leaves little time for staff to step back and focus on more-strategic issues, such as how to implement best practices. Second, posts may lack incentives to send in cases well before deadlines because late submissions can usually jump to the front of the queue. This punishes

Figure 2.6
INVEST Late Submissions as a Percentage of All Cases

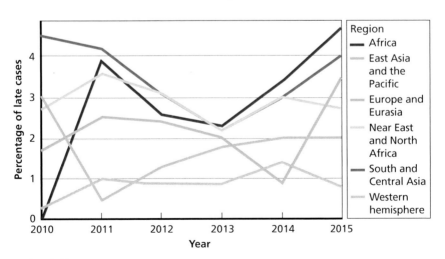

posts that follow good processes and rewards posts that have not implemented effective vetting procedures.

Gaps in Data in INVEST

INVEST is not set up to track whether training events were executed, canceled, or postponed. Thus, although we found relatively little anecdotal evidence that Leahy vetting challenges were resulting in significant numbers of training cancellations, we were unable to assess the impact of vetting on training events and other assistance. DoS personnel confirmed to us that the updated "INVEST 2.0" also will not allow linking cases to training events.[15] INVEST can report status of vetting but not whether the training occurred (although, presumably, training sponsors at post and, possibly, CCMDs at least informally keeping track in the short term). Failure to document events in an easy-to-aggregate manner makes it difficult for stakeholders to assess the number of training events that were canceled or postponed as a result of Leahy vetting.

It is important to note that, although INVEST uses 26 drop-down Title 10 (DoD) and Title 22 (DoS) funding categories, it does not aggregate and sort them according to whether they are Title 10 or Title 22 cases, which makes it difficult for DoD stakeholders to analyze and assess successes, challenges, and opportunities relevant to implementation of the DoD Leahy law specifically. It also hinders evidence-based discussions within DoD, between DoD and DoS, and between DoD and Congress.

Remediation

Remediation is the process by which partner nations take corrective action regarding ineligible units tainted with GVHR to regain eligibility for DoD-funded and DoS-funded assistance. Despite the development of a joint DoS-DoD remediation policy in February 2015 and successful efforts in such places as Afghanistan, Mexico, Guyana, and Georgia, many DoD stakeholders expressed reluctance to undertake

---

[15] Interview with U.S. officials, January 2016.

remediation.[16] Furthermore, only one of the 16 post Leahy vetting SOPs we examined addressed remediation standards.

Feedback on the clarity of remediation guidance from interviewees was mixed, with interviewees assessments of the guidance ranging from "very clear" to "no remediation standards."[17] Several interviewees said that the current remediation standards—or how they are interpreted by DoS headquarters and employed in practice—are extremely difficult to meet. One embassy-level interviewee described the remediation process as "near impossible."[18]

The difficulties with gaining acceptance of remediation have made many stakeholders across government involved in the Leahy vetting process wary of moving forward with it. For example, one CCMD's request for remediation nominations from embassies has gone unanswered since 2013.[19]

Some personnel interviewed for this report identified the ineligibility of units with older violations for remediation as an issue.[20] Even units with GVHRs occurring more than ten years ago and that had complete turnovers of personnel and practice in that time were perceived to be unable to be remediated because of the specific remediation criteria. Embassy-level interviewees contended that this keeps the United States from working with valuable partners and encouraging good behavior and transparency and suggested new policies or guidance from DoS headquarters on remediating older units.[21]

On the other hand, several embassies—with the support of their CCMDs—have begun to succeed in remediation efforts. Countries that have successfully remediated units, such as Mexico, Afghanistan, Georgia, and Guyana, started with a long-term commitment to suc-

---

[16] Interview with U.S. official, July 2016.

[17] Interviews with U.S. officials, April and May 2016.

[18] Interview with U.S. official, March 2016.

[19] Interview with U.S. officials, March 2016.

[20] Interviews with U.S. officials, March and April 2016.

[21] Interviews with U.S. officials, March and April 2016.

cessfully remediating units.[22] A willingness to invest leadership attention and staff time in the process and to engage in an iterative dialogue with officials at DoS and DoD headquarters were best practices that proved crucial to success.[23]

Time Lines for Vetting

Vetting Initial Input-to-Determination Time Lines

Data limitations required us to rely on anecdotes to analyze the amount of time the Leahy vetting process actually takes from the submission of a batch of data to INVEST until the embassy receives a determination from Washington. Our embassy interviewees said that Leahy vetting, from initial input until receipt of a final determination, could range from two to 42 days.

Our analysis of post Leahy vetting SOPs found that the time prescribed for vetting ranged from 10 business days to 6 to 8 weeks. Most SOPs reported that DoS-level vetting required 10 days, with one reporting 15 days.

One interviewee in a fast-track country estimated determination for a project with what we categorized as a moderate amount ($1 million to $20 million) of military and police aid could be made in two to three days.[24] But another said a determination of such a project would take three weeks.[25]

Most interviewees at other posts noted that DoS vetting usually occurred within seven to 14 days of the event. Several embassy interviewees noted that advance submission of vetting batches failed to speed up the determination from DoS headquarters.

---

[22] Interviews with U.S. officials, March 2016.

[23] Interviews with U.S. officials, July 2016.

[24] Interview with U.S. official, March 2016. Fast-track countries are vetted only at the embassy level and do not involve DoS headquarters vetters. Fast-track designation is determined by DoS and is granted to "functional democracies without a record of human rights abuse" Serafino et al., 2014.

[25] Interview with U.S. official, March 2016.

Delays and Bottlenecks

Most embassy-level interviewees reported that vetting time lines were not a significant issue or a major cause of canceled events. Some interviewees, however, had encountered significant delays and bottlenecks in the Leahy vetting process involving partner nations, post, and DoS headquarters.

Partner-Nation Delays

Six posts reported that delays are most commonly due to partner nations providing late or incomplete information or to information requiring additional clarification.[26] Information requiring clarification or completion often includes ranks and positions, dates of birth, and other personally identifiable information.

Delays and Bottlenecks at Post

Interviewees noted that delays within a post may result from late or incomplete submissions from sections, priority taskings overtaking Leahy vetting duties; periods with a high volume of training events; or technical issues, such as INVEST or consular database outages.[27] Researching and adjudicating DI allegations also caused delays, either because insufficient time was built into submission time lines to account for this potential requirement or because research and adjudication time stretched out over many days.[28] On the other hand, some interviewees noted that resolving an issue at the embassy could often be worth a delay, particularly when there is strong communication among stakeholders. For example, DoS and DoD officials at an embassy could research and discuss questionable reports of DI before entering a potentially problematic case into the system. As discussed later, this is especially important because DoS has not always included DoD officials in deliberations about whether information is credible once vetting moves to DoS headquarters.[29] Our analysis of post SOPs found that one post sought

---

[26] Interviews with U.S. officials, March 2016.

[27] Interviews with U.S. officials, April and May 2016.

[28] Interview with U.S. official, March 2016.

[29] Interviews with U.S. officials, March and July 2016.

to limit late submissions by requiring deputy chief of mission approval for the embassy to process the late case and forward it to Washington.

DoS Headquarters Delays

Some interviewees referenced vetting backlogs at DoS headquarters, often likely due to high volume. One interviewee noted that this appeared to be a seasonal issue.[30] While vetting determinations were largely reported to be received in time for training events, interviewees noted close calls. Some interviewees expressed concern that DoS might delay discussions on politically contentious cases, resulting in last-minute announcements of decisions. One interviewee alleged that DoS headquarters intentionally "let the clock run out" on a potentially contentious case.[31]

Short-Fuse Requests

DRL's 2012 guide on vetting policy and process requires a minimum of ten working days for vetting to take place in Washington. It advises posts to plan adequate lead time for vetting at post and in Washington to increase "the probability of successfully vetting candidates in time for their training or assistance."[32] However, short-fuse requests do occur, sometimes because of last-minute training opportunities or filling short-notice school quotas, but sometimes because of questions that arise over a candidate. Embassy-level staff members reported that DoS headquarters vetters mostly accommodated short-fuse requests, including large batches, and noted that close coordination between post and DoS headquarters is required for successful short-suspense vetting requests.[33]

Importantly, we also found evidence that, for some DoD Leahy law cases, posts do not always alert CCMD and DoS headquarters staffs, and these staffs do not always alert Pentagon staff to potential problems in advance, resulting in short-fuse situations in Washington.

---

[30] Interviews with U.S. officials, March and May 2016.

[31] Interview with U.S. official, May 2016.

[32] DoS, 2012, p. 12.

[33] Interviews with U.S. officials, March, April, and May 2016.

Despite efforts to proactively address problematic vetting cases well before training deadlines, communication shortfalls mean that there is not always sufficient time to analyze and deliberate over difficult cases in Washington.[34]

Clarity of Scope for Vetting

Defining What Constitutes DoD Assistance

While the guidance on what programs and activity types are subject to Leahy vetting is relatively clear, our interviews indicated that the challenge lies in translating this guidance into action. Interviewees cited difficulties in determining which programs and events required vetting, in part because of uncertainties about whether activities met the definitions of "training or other assistance." Embassy personnel particularly cited activities funded by the Asia Pacific Regional Initiative (APRI) and Traditional CCMD Activities (TCA) as those for which it is unclear whether vetting is required.[35] Other interviewees, however, noted that their guidance is clear: APRI activities that involve training, equipment, or other assistance should be vetted, while TCA events do not need to be vetted, since they are not supposed to involve training. Nevertheless, one CCMD interviewee stated that they frequently find (and remove) training activities that are planned as part of TCA events.[36]

While most interviewees affirmed that they follow specific formal guidance in determining which programs require vetting, the source of guidance cited varied. DoS officials generally cited guidance from DRL. DoD officials cited either the 2014 SECDEF memo, guidance from the CCMD, DRL guidance, or a combination of these three sources. Our analysis of post SOPs found that only one of the 16 SOPs examined provided a list of specific programs that require vet-

---

[34] Interviews with U.S. officials, September and December 2015 and February, April, and July 2016.

[35] Interviews with U.S. officials, March and April 2016.

[36] Interview with U.S. official, March 2016.

ting. Interviewees also reported reaching out to both DoS and DoD for clarification on issues related to vetting only to receive conflicting guidance. In one example, DoS provided guidance that vetting was not required for some military personnel to attend conferences, but DoD informed the post that select conferences necessitated vetting.[37] Such issues may arise from the differences in Title 10 and Title 22 programs and provisions, as well as the possibility that DoD officials may sometimes want to err on the side of caution.

Both prior research and our interviews provided evidence that, while it is generally clear which programs require vetting, occasional challenges lie in a lack of clarity about security cooperation authorities and policies writ large. For example, TCA events are authorized to promote military-to-military engagement, not training. Yet security cooperation planners sometimes propose an event that blurs the line between basic engagement and familiarization activities and more rigorous training. If DoD were to conduct a TCA event that strayed into the realm of training, it could inadvertently violate the Leahy Law, even though DoD guidance says TCA events do not require vetting. Some CCMD staffs we interviewed preempt this problem by subjecting all proposals for TCA events to a rigorous legal review to ensure no training is involved. Requiring such a legal review is clearly an important best practice, to prevent violations of both the Leahy law and the Antideficiency Act (which prohibits the expenditure of funds for purposes not authorized by Congress).[38]

Determining Vetting Requirements at Post

Our interviews suggest that more clarity on scope of vetting is required, perhaps through some combination of guidance, improved communication, and training. Interpretations as to which programs, individuals, and units required vetting varied widely. The interviews found DoD officials and those conducting or overseeing the vetting at the post are unclear on when the process is required. Several interviewees in a wide variety of posts said they were aware of programs excluded from vet-

---

[37] Interview with U.S. official, May 2016.

[38] The Antideficiency Act, PL 97–258, 96 Stat. 923.

ting but cited a perception of risk in using these and opting to vet instead.[39] It is worth noting that these programs are not exempt from vetting; rather, the Leahy law does not require vetting for them. Some events, such as subject-matter expert exchanges, were highlighted as not requiring vetting, because they do not involve training.[40]

Given the occasional confusion about desired scope of vetting, embassy-level interviewees reported three primary approaches to determine whether to vet: (1) defer to program owners, (2) utilize a rule of thumb, and (3) vet all individuals or units regardless of program, event, or even funding source. It is worth noting that these practices may sometimes provide embassies some flexibility in deciding how strictly to apply DoD and DoS guidance but at other times might create new challenges, such as overburdening the vetting system.

Defer to Program Owners

Several of our interviews demonstrate reliance on the embassy section that "owns" the program or event, or on the political section, which "owns" the Leahy vetting process at post. Two Leahy vetting coordinators said they simply defer to the embassy section that owns the program or activity to determine whether vetting is required.[41] One acknowledged that he is not certain that everything that should be vetted is but that he has no evidence that anyone who should not have received training has had training.

Utilize a Rule of Thumb

Officials at five embassies reported using a rule of thumb. For example, they will vet if U.S. taxpayer dollars "touch an event," vet if the U.S. pays for partner transportation to an event, or vet military personnel but not civilians for all events.[42] This includes programs, such as APRI,

---

[39] Confusion over exempt programs exists; for example, a U.S. official interviewed for this report incorrectly identified a program as not requiring Leahy vetting (interview with U.S. official, February 2016). Reports of purposefully vetting for programs exempt from vetting include interviews with U.S. officials, March and May 2016.

[40] Interviews with U.S. officials, March 2016.

[41] Interviews with U.S. officials, March 2016.

[42] Interviews with U.S. officials, March and May 2016.

for which vetting is not always required.[43] Interviewees also reported relying on the political section to set a rule of thumb to define whether vetting is required. Some posts, given the lack of guidance and clarification from DoS or DoD, have created definitions based on their interpretation of the law. For example, one embassy in Europe requires vetting of any military or security forces who have the power to arrest or detain.[44]

Vet Everything

Another common strategy employed by the four embassies we examined is vetting all activities, regardless of funding sources.[45] This strategy appears to be more common with countries that are designated as fast track, that report a low volume of vetting, or that see their internal vetting process as particularly effective. In one such country, the vet-everything strategy even includes vetting when the partner nation spends its own money on U.S. training.[46] Another interviewee noted that his post went as far as to vet individuals who were part of previously approved units for each event.[47] One embassy coined the term *courtesy vetting* for its additional vetting.

Information Used for Vetting

Sources of Information

DRL mandates that embassies use the INVEST Database and Document Library, which contain information from past vetting. It also advises embassies to "use as many reliable and credible sources of information as are available," including embassy files, Regional Security Office records, the Consular Lookout and Support System, the records of the law enforcement agencies and DoD offices at post, and

---

[43] Interview with U.S. official, March 2016.

[44] Interviews with U.S. officials, March 2016.

[45] Interviews with U.S. officials, March 2016.

[46] Interview with U.S. official, March 2016.

[47] Interview with U.S. official, April 2016.

the Internet and outreach to local human rights NGOs, government officials, and media contacts.[48] When conducting vetting, the DRL guide suggests tips for effective searches, such as using multiple variations of a name, trying different search terms, and conducting additional searches if DI is vague or unreliable.[49]

The primary sources of information cited by embassy-level staff and DoS officials involved in the vetting process are embassy databases (including the consular system referenced above), newspaper articles, reports by NGOs and human rights organizations, and information received by partner nations related to the specific event. Many interviewees referenced keeping internal databases of GVHR violators—both at the individual and unit level—to ensure compliance with Leahy-vetting standards.[50] One interviewee noted using contact with partner-nation counterparts and official partner-government documents, such as organizational charts, to disprove alleged DI.[51]

Defining Credible Information

Many of our interviewees noted concerns about the sources used to determine vetting outcomes or support DI findings. One interviewee described a hierarchy of information sources, terming official reporting as "reliable," other media as "mixed," and social media as "very fuzzy."[52] Concerns include issues with NGOs' and human rights organizations' reporting, particularly reports from questionable sources that tarnish whole units and organizations as GVHR abusers.[53]

DoS guidance provides a definition of credible information, but many interviewees continue to express confusion or disagreement with how the guidance is implemented. Our analysis of 16 post SOPs found that only one defined credible information. One interviewee

---

[48] DoS, 2012.

[49] DoS, 2012.

[50] Interviews with U.S. officials, March, April, and May 2016.

[51] Interview with U.S. official, May 2016.

[52] Interview with U.S. officials, March 2017.

[53] Interviews with U.S. officials, March, April, and May 2016.

requested a clarification from DoS headquarters and was told it was up to the post.[54] Interviewees reported a significant difference between their posts' definition of credible information and the standard vetters at DoS headquarters used. Many of our interviewees felt that potentially untrustworthy information, such as allegations from questionable sources, was weighed and valued differently within different levels of the Leahy vetting process. For example, one DoS official noted that the evidentiary threshold for credible information was relatively low.[55] Stakeholders perceived final determinations on information credibility to be opaque and inconsistent. This was frustrating not only for DoD officials implementing assistance programs but also for the partners themselves. As one CCMD official noted: "Failure to apply appropriate rigor to adjudication prior to the suspension of assistance may negatively impact bilateral relationships and partner nation willingness to investigate and address legitimate allegations."[56]

Interviewees expressed concern that DoS headquarters taking questionable GVHR allegations at face value could taint clean units based on false information. In one example, GVHR abuses by a security force were alleged by a large human rights advocacy organization. The post was able to leverage existing relationships with the partner government and in-country NGOs to provide DoS headquarters with background to refute these allegations. The interviewee noted that, without the extensive efforts of embassy staff, DoS could have easily moved the security force into a tainted area based on false information.[57] Vague allegations could taint whole organizations or several units, particularly if the violation was only perpetrated by select individuals.[58] Embassy-level interviewees noted that they undertook significant additional work to disprove allegations DoS headquarters

[54] Interview with U.S. official, April 2016.

[55] Interview with U.S. official, March 2016.

[56] DoD, 2016.

[57] Interview with U.S. officials, March 2016.

[58] Interview with U.S. official, March 2016.

highlighted to prevent unnecessary tainting of units or individuals.[59] An interviewee reported spending months researching GVHR allegations against military personnel because the allegations excluded large swaths of the military from training, despite the lack of an official determination from DoS. She was able to identify discrepancies in the allegations and issued a cable refuting them, which paved the way for the personnel to be vetted again.[60]

Determining Other Derogatory Information and Final Decisions

Our analysis of post SOPs found that found that 11 defined *GVHR* and seven defined the term *other derogatory information*. The definitions provided were found to be consistent with DRL guidance.

In our discussions of many vetting cases, we found evidence that the other derogatory information might not actually involve human rights violations but still adversely affected the Leahy vetting process. For example, such violations as driving under the influence of alcohol, which could result in visa ineligibility, were also used to suspend assistance to individuals and units. Indeed, several interviewees noted issues with DI related to visa ineligibilities; while these individuals are still eligible to be vetted, they might not be able to attend the event. In these cases, although the Leahy vetting process is the vehicle for vetting individuals, they are not approved for training for policy reasons rather than because approving them is explicitly forbidden by the Leahy law. This distinction between legal and policy-driven choices is sometimes lost on stakeholders. Three interviewees reported using the *"New York Times* front-page test" as a rule of thumb: If the DI could make the front page of a major newspaper, then the vetting should be suspended.[61]

Our analysis of the process—reinforced by many interviews— indicated that DoD and embassy-level stakeholders are often not included in the final stages of case deliberations and determinations. DoS headquarters decisionmaking about some cases may suffer from

---

[59] Interviews with U.S. officials, March and May 2016.

[60] Interview with U.S. official, May 2016.

[61] Interviews with U.S. officials, March 2016.

inadequate dialogue, perhaps due to a combination of deadline pressures, limited governance structures, and competing demands on staff time. In terms of transparency, once DoS headquarters makes a decision, nonapprovals are not always adequately explained, resulting in significant frustration among both U.S. and partner officials.[62]

Issues with Country-Specific Information

Several embassy-level staff raised questions about the reliability of information received from partner nations, even basic information, such as an individual's name, date of birth, place of birth, gender, rank, and job title. At one post, an estimated 25 percent of the data received from the partner nation required further investigation.[63]

The 2012 DRL vetting guide acknowledges that embassies vary in resources and that the security forces of partner nations vary in the levels of available historic and demographic information. Thus, the information used to vet at the embassy level may vary by country. Several interviewees based in Africa and the Middle East noted issues stemming from naming conventions and common names, resulting in false identification of DI.[64]

Interviewees also noted issues resulting from variation in the translation and standardization of military ranks and positions.[65] Among the workarounds they reported to these issues were providing detailed guidance in English and other languages to the partner nation, researching the partner-nation's military structure to correctly translate rank and positions, and creating forms for the partner military to complete.[66]

---

[62] Interview with U.S. official, March 2016.

[63] Interviews with U.S. officials, March and April 2016.

[64] Other regional embassy staff reported issues with names; interviews with U.S. officials, March and April 2016.

[65] Interviews with U.S. officials, March and May 2016.

[66] Interviews with U.S. officials, March 2016.

Adequacy of Training and Staff Resources for Vetting

Training

Only one-quarter of embassy-level interviewees (both DoD and DoS) possessed previous experience with Leahy vetting prior to their current positions. Interviewees said that who had training at post was unclear and that they often guessed who received training and what it entailed.[67] Our analysis of post SOPs found that only four embassies direct or require personnel who use INVEST to take the Foreign Service Institute's distance learning course on the system (PP410 INVEST: Leahy Vetting at Post).

Five of the 12 embassy-level DoD personnel we interviewed reported receiving formal training on Leahy vetting. Three reported receiving training at Defense Security Cooperation Agency's ISCS prior to reporting to post. Another reported completing the Foreign Service Institute online course at post. A fifth reported attending a training session at his post conducted by a Leahy vetter visiting from Washington. The other DoD personnel we interviewed reported on-the-job training and turnover as their primary means of learning about the Leahy-vetting process. As one embassy security cooperation officer termed it, training is largely "word of mouth and tradition."[68]

While several interviewees thought the training adequate, others who received formal training largely viewed the training programs as inadequate. Several CCMD and regional DoS staff members also noted the inadequacy of training. Both ISCS and the Foreign Service Institute course focus on the content of Leahy vetting but not on the Leahy vetting process or the INVEST system.[69] Both DoD and DoS officials expressed an interest in joint training or seeing the materials provided to the other as background.[70]

---

[67] Interviews with U.S. officials, March and May 2016.

[68] Interviews with U.S. officials, March 2016.

[69] Interview with U.S. official, March 2016.

[70] Interview with U.S. official, March 2016.

Staffing

In nine embassies at which we conducted interviews for this report, DoD programs generate the preponderance of vetting requests. The 2014 CRS report on Leahy vetting acknowledged that a lack of resources dedicated to vetting may be a challenge. It highlighted the critiques of observers that vetting operations at some embassies may be understaffed due to a lack of dedicated funding for Leahy vetting.[71] We found that two of 18 embassies had staff dedicated full time exclusively to Leahy vetting. The others surveyed had staff with collateral duties related to Leahy vetting. Nevertheless, no embassy reported the amount of staffing dedicated to Leahy vetting to be inadequate at post.

Several interviewees did note staffing issues related to part-time duties and periods of high activity. Both embassy-level and DoS headquarters staff noted that posts require either additional or full-time staff working on Leahy-vetting issues to reduce bottlenecks and delays.[72] Because Leahy vetting is a secondary duty, many staff reported that vetting duties fall by the wayside during high-level visits and other events. One example is an embassy official with secondary duties as the Leahy vetting coordinator at post "going dark" during a congressional delegation visit.[73] Interviewees also reported busy periods related to the timing of trainings and exercises when additional staff would be helpful. In some embassies, backup staffers—embassy staffers identified and trained in advance—are used to when high volumes of batches are being produced.[74]

The role of foreign service nationals, often referred to as *locally employed staff*, in the Leahy vetting process has been contentious in at least one case, based on the theory that they may have a conflict of interest when searching for personal information on fellow citizens.[75] According to many other interviewees, however, they play a signifi-

---

[71] CRS, 2014, p. 13.

[72] Interviews with U.S. officials, March 2016.

[73] Interview with U.S. officials, March 2016.

[74] Interview with U.S. official, April 2016.

[75] Interview with U.S. official, February 2016.

cant role in data collection and batch submission and, in some cases, first-stage vetting.[76] Locally employed staff, particularly those working with DoD security cooperation officers, appear to handle most data-entry duties. Many interviewees noted how this aids the workflow of the embassy-side process and the difficulty they would have without data entry help during busy periods.[77] CCMD staff members reported the provision of INVEST access to locally employed staff as a helpful development.[78]

Many of our embassy-level interviews noted the heavy workloads of DoS headquarters Leahy vetters and of DoD and DoS staff involved in program oversight.

Training and Staffing at CCMDs

With the exceptions of USSOUTHCOM and USNORTHCOM, CCMDs lacked the training and staffing to play an effective, proactive role supporting DoD efforts to implement Leahy and to integrate human rights considerations into security cooperation more generally. At USSOUTHCOM and USNORTHCOM, implementation of Leahy laws was seen as just one component of a broader effort to promote human rights, and other CCMD staffs focused on meeting the letter of the Leahy law. All CCMD staffs emphasized that Leahy vetting was managed at embassies, but USSOUTHCOM and USNORTH-COM appeared to provide far more robust and sophisticated support to embassies and to overseers in Washington, D.C.

Partner Relationships

Challenges and Best Practices in Obtaining Information

Interviewees reported difficulty in obtaining information from partner nations. One embassy-level staff member noted that the biggest challenge was explaining why certain information—personally identifiable

---

[76] Interviews with U.S. officials, March 2016.

[77] Interviews with U.S. officials, March 2016.

[78] Interview with U.S. officials, March 2016.

information or information disproving potential DI—was necessary, without harming the bilateral relationship.[79] Embassy interviews highlighted frustration at the lack of available partner-nation organizational information, which otherwise might have reduced the spread of taint, and the difficulty in recreating this information through research.[80]

In addition to partner nations withholding information, such practices as poor record management, unique military structures, naming conventions, and tracking personally identifiable information frustrate the Leahy vetting process.

In the FY 2014 DoD report to Congress, USNORTHCOM highlighted a best practice for both improving partner trust and facilitating information sharing: The U.S. Office of Defense Cooperation in Mexico had established biweekly coordination meetings with its Mexican counterparts to increase transparency on vetting cases.[81]

Maintaining Diplomatic and Military-to-Military Relationships

Denial of training, particularly without a comprehensive explanation, is politically sensitive. One interviewee explained that tensions arose with the partner nation after a "golden boy" within the military was tied to DI and suspended from training. The embassy was unable to provide details, further upsetting high-ranking military officials.[82] In one example, a unit with a "one-year approval" was repeatedly falsely accused of GVHR by the press, resulting in the suspension of all training to this unit and harming the military-to-military relationship with the partner nation. This incident created additional tension between DoD and DoS, as it was elevated by the post to the CCMD and OSD.[83]

Canceled trainings and events were also reported to upset partner nations. An embassy-level staff member reported that his post canceled

---

[79] Interview with U.S. official, March 2016.

[80] Interview with U.S. official, May 2016.

[81] DoD, 2015.

[82] Interview with U.S. official, March 2016.

[83] Interview with U.S. official, April 2016.

25 training events with the military partner due to the suspension and rejection of participants, which strained the bilateral relationship.[84]

---

[84] Interview with U.S. official, April 2016.

CHAPTER THREE

Key Findings and Recommendations

In Chapter One, we presented the six research questions that shaped our analytic approach. From our analysis of prior reports and from personal interviews we conducted with Leahy vetters and other officials involved in the vetting process, we developed the findings and recommendations highlighted below. While many of these findings and recommendations may apply to both DoS and DoD, we focus primarily on how they might help DoD—especially OSD—to build its capacity for effective and efficient human rights vetting.

Findings

Process: Leahy Vetting Requirements Are Generally Not a Roadblock to Security Assistance, but Inadequate Governance Structures Make Oversight Challenging

Based on our review of guidance and other documents, as well as our wide range of interviews, we found that the Leahy vetting process has improved over time but continues to create challenges and frustrations. Although several interviewees argued that an excessive number of training events are canceled due to problems in the Leahy vetting process, we could not find evidence to support these claims. Indeed, many more interviewees argued that, although the system could be challenging, its weaknesses and inefficiencies rarely derailed planned training or other assistance. At least two DoD combatant commanders in recent years have requested but found little evidence of significant problems caused by the Leahy vetting process, despite hearing complaints to the contrary.[1] On the other hand, as discussed in Chapter Three, many DoD stakeholders did not feel that DoD was a full partner in the vetting process, despite the need for a full partnership in the execution of DoD Leahy law implementation.

INVEST data—when combined with interviews—also indicated that, overall, vetting did not significantly block security assistance efforts. For the five years between 2011 and 2015 (starting with the first full year for which INVEST data enable comprehensive analysis and ending with the most recent full year), fewer than 0.3 percent of proposed cases were rejected; 90.7 percent had been approved; and the remaining 9 percent were suspended or canceled. Many interviewees said most individuals and units that were not approved were replaced by other candidates so that DoD could still provide promised assistance.

The Leahy process can be cumbersome and complicated—and is operated by officials for whom it is very rarely a full-time job. Embassy SOPs are sometimes helpful but sometimes have significant gaps. As a result, officials sometimes devise practices to make the system operate more smoothly. Many of these are valuable, for example, officials phoning a colleague for quick consultation rather than working through a lengthy bureaucratic process for review of potential DI. However, the thousands of times vetters suspend or cancel cases and then have to scramble to replace these individuals with backups stresses the system, strains the capacity of vetters, and creates uncertainty and frustration among U.S. assistance providers and their partners. Through the dedicated efforts of embassy and Washington officials, mission failure is usually avoided, but it can sometimes feel unnecessarily hard. In both the FY 2014 and FY 2015 DoD reports to Congress, U.S. Africa Command reported that "self-screening" by U.S. and partner nations occurs, meaning that only units and individuals likely to meet vetting requirements are nominated. Self-screening reportedly occurs "not only in cases where there has been a gross violation of human rights, but also in cases where partners have grown frustrated with our pro-

---

[1]   Interviews with U.S. officials, January and March 2016.

cesses, and when allegations of limited credibility are judged too difficult or time consuming to disapprove."[2]

The introduction of a category of "cancellation" in addition to "suspension" in 2014 provides a useful example of both the benefits and unintended consequences of process changes. Until 2014, Leahy vetters had only three options: Accept, reject, or suspend, with "suspend" serving as a de facto work-around for almost every case that could not be speedily accepted or rejected. This kept the process wheels turning but left the suspended individuals or units (between 7.7 and 9.0 percent annually) in limbo: Should they be regarded as provisionally tainted or merely as victims of bureaucratic time lines? To mitigate this confusion, vetters have, since 2014, been permitted to cancel a case—without prejudice to the candidate—if it could not be completed for administrative reasons.

In theory, this should have brought clarity to the system. In practice, however, cancellation simply took over most of the space formerly occupied by suspension. A closer look at the data presented in Chapter Two, shows that the bulk of nonacceptances (over 85 percent of 18,729 such cases in 2015) are now cancellations.[3] It is not always clear to either U.S. or partner officials what is really behind suspension and cancellation decisions, and while such steps might prevent cancellation of a particular event, confusion and bad feelings sometimes remain.

Such work-arounds, self-screening, suspension, and cancellation, give vetters a way to keep events on schedule or avoid making hard (and at times politically awkward) decisions under tight schedules. This has obvious attractions—but also creates confusion as to the meaning of Leahy determinations. Although case rejections and event cancellations are reduced, a 9 percent suspension or cancellation rate for units and individuals should not necessarily be considered successful. Rather than seeing the Leahy vetting process described in Chapter One as a series of collaborative, dynamic, human rights–focused deliberations, most stakeholders perceive it as an assembly line of sorts. Questions are

---

[2] DoD, 2015. See also DoD, 2016.

[3] RAND analysis of INVEST data. Total cases 2011–2014: 641,156, total rejections 2,079 (3.24 percent); total cases 2015: 182,969, total rejections 284 (1.55 percent).

left unanswered and learning opportunities missed to keep the process moving. Rather than being able to focus on long-term policy issues and proactively shape Leahy vetting for the future, DoS and DoD overseers spend much of their energy managing the assembly line and responding to problematic cases against tight deadlines. Simply put, Leahy implementation lacks a robust, well-structured governance process with a series of regular check-ins among a range of DoS and DoD stakeholders at both the working and leadership levels.

Process: The Leahy Vetting Process Should Be Made More Transparent to DoD Stakeholders

DoD has always had a role in the Leahy vetting process, and that role was strengthened and clarified through the 2012 and 2014 guidance described in Chapter One. Nevertheless, many interviewees expressed concerns about their limited role and the lack of transparency in the system. A better understanding of how the process works and their ability to influence that process would enable DoD to benefit from tools its staff possess but often do not use effectively. With more forward-leaning action, DoD staff could prevent a lot of last-minute scrambling to fill training slots; replace units or individuals whose cases have been rejected, suspended, or canceled; and ensure that security assistance activities can be completed on schedule.

A great deal of the confusion surrounding Leahy vetting stems from the system's complexity—and from the lack of clear, transparent, consistent communication among all DoS and DoD stakeholders. The DoS guideline document published in 2012, which remains the most authoritative DoS description of the process, is 64 pages long.[4] The flow chart setting out only the DoS portion of the process fills three pages. Detailed guidance is an important foundation for effective processes, but without a robust, inclusive governance process to facilitate communication, the formal guidance can be daunting and can create a feeling among stakeholders that they do not have avenues for engaging in a meaningful dialogue once their own initial steps have been completed. To many DoD observers, the process looks like a black box.

---

[4]   DoS, 2012.

Efforts to supplement formal guidance with additional means of sharing information would improve understanding of the process and help demystify it. Some DoD interviewees perceived the system as described in Figure 3.1, with a process in which DoD hands off a case to DoS for final decision rather than a collaborative effort from start to finish.

As discussed in Chapter One, GAO portrayed the system more accurately,[5] but even that did not adequately highlight the fact that DoD officials can and should play a role at every step of the Leahy vetting process. At the embassy level, DoD officials should engage in iterative dialogue with their DoS counterparts for problematic cases, drawing in CCMD staff, as needed. At the headquarters level, OSD and Joint Staff officials should have a more formalized governance structure that holds regular meetings at both the working and executive levels. These meetings could discuss both individual problematic cases and broader policy issues, drawing in CCMD and embassy staff, as needed.

Improved communication may increase transparency. While some DoS headquarters officials argued that they were constantly in com-

Figure 3.1
Common Misperception of Leahy Vetting Process

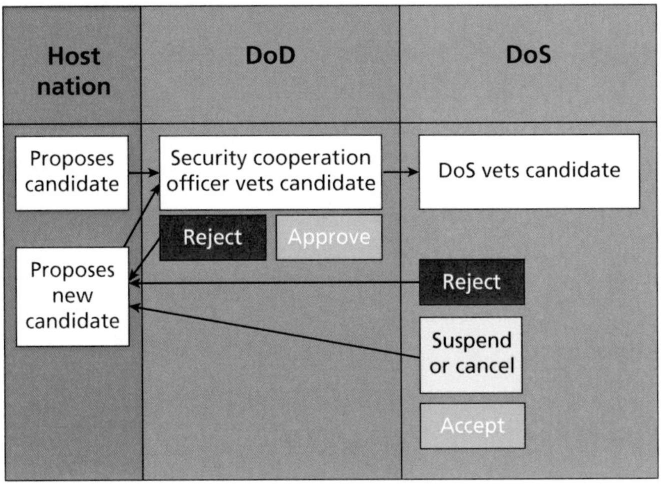

RAND *RR1737-3.1*

---

5   GAO, 2013.

munication with stakeholders about the full range of Leahy vetting details from the broadest strategic goals to the finest details of implementation, other stakeholders asserted that feedback was sometimes lacking, and still others felt completely in the dark. In the same way that Figure 3.1 underemphasizes the role of DoD, some DoD interviewees at embassies felt they had no voice in the process (or visibility into the process) beyond recommending a name or unit.

Our analysis identified a need for better communication about the purpose, process, and outcomes of Leahy vetting. As discussed at the start of this report, the Leahy laws serve a purpose central to American values: the protection of human rights around the world. While this report focuses on process and implementation issues, it was clear from our analysis that stakeholders who fully understood the purpose of Leahy vetting were more motivated and more effective at managing implementation. Thus, leaders at every level of DoS and DoD would benefit from communicating the value of Leahy vetting for American interests and being transparent about both good news stories and cautionary tales.

In terms of communicating about the process itself, DoS DRL, regional bureau, and embassy officials do not always operate in concert, while at DoD the communication among security cooperation officers, CCMDs, and the Pentagon varies greatly. Rather than a transparent, multi-stakeholder governance process, many interviewees saw a more ad hoc, personality-based means of communication.

Many stakeholders also found it difficult to have a voice in—or even visibility into—the final outcomes of Leahy vetting efforts, arguing that many deliberations were conducted behind closed doors. In addition to a perceived lack of a transparent governance process, interviewees also expressed concern that it is too hard for people with a vested interest in the Leahy process and vetting decisions to get access to INVEST and related information.

Process: Gaps Exist in the INVEST System

There appear to be some challenges using the INVEST system to support policy analysis. Neither the RAND team nor several DoD officials were able to determine through INVEST how cases linked to training events, making it difficult to know, for example, how often non-approved cases led to cancelled events. Although embassies share rosters of proposed participants for particular events and non-approval notes in INVEST explain decisions, the event information is difficult to aggregate at a higher level. Thus, while INVEST meets the immediate, narrowly focused requirement to support vetting of individuals and units, it lacks context that can be important for DoD and other stakeholders to conduct strategic analysis.

Secondly, as discussed in Chapter Two, although INVEST uses 26 drop-down DoS and DoD funding categories, it has no Title 10 (DoD) vs. Title 22 (DoS) sorting or aggregating function, which makes it difficult to analyze implementation of the DoD Leahy law. This makes it difficult to analyze and assess successes, challenges, and opportunities relevant to implementation of the DoD Leahy law (which applies to Title 10 events). It also hinders evidence-based discussions on Title 10–related vetting among DoD, DoS, and Congress.

Process: Remediation for a Tainted Unit Requires Leadership Commitment and an Iterative Dialogue

As discussed in Chapter One, the introduction of remediation guidance in 2015 provided a tool to help partner nations improve their human rights records, rather than merely punish offenders after the fact—a goal Assistant Secretary of State Tom Malinowski for Democracy, Human Rights and Labor described as "the whole point of the Leahy law."[6] But many Leahy implementers are wary of the remediation process as a means of drawing partner nations more in line with U.S. objectives.

Some stakeholders have argued that the remediation process is too cumbersome and that relevant information is too difficult to obtain.[7] Nevertheless, best practices now exist, and there may be opportunities to use informal guidance and information-sharing forums to supplement existing formal guidance and thus help others start the process. For example, in such places as USNORTHCOM and the U.S.

---

[6] Egozi, 2016

[7] See, for example, DoD, 2016; interview with U.S. official, July 2016.

embassy in Mexico, a willingness to invest leadership attention and staff time in the process and to engage in an iterative dialogues with officials at DoS and DoD headquarters were best practices that proved crucial to success.

Process: Leahy Vetting Appears to Be Relatively Effective at Weeding out Past and Potential Human Rights Violators

Although a few concerns have been raised publicly,[8] we found little evidence that Leahy vetting either fails to identify human rights violators or that Leahy-vetted units or individuals go on to commit abuses later. That said, a lack of systematic record keeping on subsequent abuse findings or allegations against Leahy-vetted units meant that our analysis was limited to data derived from interviews. For example, one DoD official argued that Leahy vetting contributed to a drop in abuse reports filed in Mexico by more than 50 percent over the past three years.[9] Our analysis of statements and reports from human rights groups identified far more positive references to Leahy vetting efforts than evidence of failures in the system.[10] Nevertheless, 824,125 units and individuals have been cleared through the Leahy-vetting process over the past five years, but neither DoS nor DoD tracks the number of cleared cases that have subsequently faced accusations, whether for acts prior or subsequent to their vetting. A systematic mechanism for tracking such data might improve both the actual functioning of the Leahy process (e.g., by enabling vetters to learn from past mistakes and

---

[8]   U.S. Congress, "Human Rights Vetting: Nigeria and Beyond," hearing before the Subcommittee on Africa, Global Health, Global Human Rights, and International Organizations, Committee on Foreign Affairs, House of Representatives, 113th Cong., 2nd Sess., July 10, 2014; Douglas Gillison, "Moral Hazard: How the United States Trained Cambodian Human Rights Abusers, Breaking U.S. Law," 100 Reporters website, March 18, 2016; Nahal Toosi, "State Dept. assures Leahy on Israeli human rights scrutiny," Politico website, May 5, 2016.

[9]   Remarks by Deputy Assistant Secretary of Defense for Western Hemisphere Affairs Rebecca Chavez, as quoted in Egozi, 2016.

[10]   See, for example, Kathryn R. Striffolino and Nate Smith, "Deconstructing Leahy Law: Fact vs Fiction," Amnesty International website, July 9, 2013; see also Lewis Mudge, "The Executioners' Bill," Human Rights Watch website, March 26, 2015; for a contrary view, see Gillison, 2016.

to see which types of cases are more likely to fall through the system's cracks) and its perception by the public.

Timing: The Leahy Vetting Process Is Not Too Slow but Can Be Challenged by Tight Deadlines

Some interviewees claimed the vetting process can be slow, sometimes taking weeks or months, while others claimed that the average turn-around time is ten days, and many countries have an expedited clearance process. In some cases, herculean efforts by vetters expedited cases when needed, and some major cases were approved in a matter of days under tight deadlines.

Some of the practices described earlier can prevent cancellations of training events, but can also lead to two problems:

1. A deadline-focused atmosphere makes it harder to get ahead of problems and be more strategic.
2. Problems may simply be avoided by abandoning units and individuals who may need more discussion and instead using backup names so that events can go on. Important partners may then miss out on valuable training, and DoD resources might be used inefficiently on candidates who are not the best fit for that particular training. In addition, potentially clean units or individuals may be left with a taint of suspicion, and a feeling of unfair treatment.

Schedule pressures can lead to candidates being screened out before reaching DoS headquarters or canceled before adjudication on the substantive merits of the case. Many of these situations might be avoidable, particularly those turned back due to inadequate information in the initial case presentation. For example, if an individual is put forward with incomplete rank or name or if a unit is identified simply as belonging to the "Ministry of Defense," vetters will go back to the post to fill in the details but, if additional information is not forthcoming, will cancel the case. As we discuss under "Recommendations," increased training, improved communication and governance structures, and slightly longer lead times could help prevent many of these problems from arising in the first place and quickly resolve many of those that remain.

Scope: Guidance on What Programs Require Leahy Vetting Is Relatively Clear Yet Perceived as Confusing in Practice

A thorough reading of OSD's 2014 implementation guidance makes the scope of Leahy vetting requirements fairly clear.[11] Although it notes that it is not comprehensive, the guidance lists most security assistance programs and explains why they do or do not require vetting. Many stakeholders, however, stated that both the DoS and DoD guidance is confusing. Why is there a disconnect? Much of the challenge lies in determining whether an activity involves "training and other assistance," as defined in the guidance. As discussed in Chapter Two, the line between activities that do not require vetting, e.g., familiarization or interoperability, and those that do can be blurry for implementers, who sometimes mistake training for information-sharing and vice versa. Given the lack of Leahy-vetting training for many stakeholders and a desire for caution, some embassies follow a "vet everything" approach. This is valid if an embassy simply wants to apply Leahy-law principles to all foreign interactions, but it should be made clear that this is a policy decision, not a legal requirement, and that it may be a useful practice for some embassies but may also burden the vetting process.

Information Used: Determining What Constitutes Credible Information Is Often Perceived as Unclear

While most cases encounter no allegations of DI, those that do can create significant dilemmas. Several of our embassy-level interviewees noted that it is sometimes unclear to them what sources of information are most credible. This can result in bottlenecks within the process as embassy staff and others expend time determining whether the allegations are credible. Additionally, GVHR and other allegations lacking credibility run the risk of tainting otherwise clean units and thus inhibiting U.S. assistance. Understanding better how non-GVHR DI

---

[11] OSD 2014.

affects vetting is also a challenge for embassy staff. Furthermore, country-specific information obtained from partner nations is often incorrect and sometimes forces embassy staff to struggle to acquire the necessary information.

Finally, and most important, interviewees often felt they had little voice in final determinations on information credibility and perceived the process to be opaque and the determinations to be inconsistent. This was a frustration not only for DoD officials implementing assistance programs but also for the partners themselves. As one CCMD official has noted: "Failure to apply appropriate rigor to adjudication prior to the suspension of assistance may negatively impact bilateral relationships and partner nation willingness to investigate and address legitimate allegations."[12]

Training and Staff Resources: Improvements in Training May Improve Implementation Significantly

Most interviewees had no prior experience or formal training before taking on Leahy-vetting responsibilities, and most of those who had received training considered it inadequate. There were differences between DoS and DoD training, and in neither case did there seem to be a sufficient focus on managing the vetting process itself. There appeared to be a need for training not only on training in the vetting process but for more on security cooperation processes and human rights issues generally. While we found examples of innovative approaches to informal training, e.g., tips of the week and cheat sheets, DoS or DoD had made little effort to facilitate the sharing or institutionalization of these types of best practices.

Levels of dedicated staffing did not seem to be a problem among embassy staffs, despite occasional strains caused by vetting complications. The use of foreign service nationals and nonpermanent U.S. staff were key to managing workloads, although the part-time nature of Leahy-vetting responsibilities led to some concern about competing priorities. Staff dedicated to human rights issues at two CCMDs enabled a more strategic, proactive approach to supporting Leahy-law

---

[12] DoD, 2016.

implementation and promotion of human rights, which we assessed to be a best practice. Other CCMD staffs appeared to take a more hands-off, legalistic approach, which could make it harder to help shape the iterative dialogues that are necessary for DoD to be a more equal partner in the Leahy vetting process.

Partner Relationships: Improved Communication Guidance and Support Could Reduce Negative Effects of Leahy-Vetting Problems

As discussed in Chapter Two, the Leahy-vetting process can create tension between the United States and partner nations. Much of the tension, however, could be reduced if U.S. officials explained Leahy procedures better and offered support for partner nations in navigating and tracking what the can perceive as a bureaucratic maze. Embassy, CCMD, and even some senior DoD and DoS officials may avoid certain types of assistance, individuals, or units to avoid awkward discussions of Leahy requirements, even when such engagement—if done well—could strengthen relationships over the longer term.

Overuse of suspensions and cancelations and the failure to come to more definitive closure (accept or reject) on more cases may confuse partner governments. Despite definitions that differentiate suspensions from cancellations, partner officials do not necessarily know whether a candidate has substantive problems or is merely the victim of bureaucratic schedules—and embassy officials might not be eager to initiate a difficult conversation to shed light on the issue.

The U.S. government as a whole needs to improve its communication with partner nations on Leahy issues, on both substance and technicalities. Too often, partners see Leahy merely as a bureaucratic impediment and have little understanding of *their* role in creating a smooth process. An open and honest discussion about problematic cases—not merely those rejected but also those suspended with prejudice or canceled prior to adjudication—would help partner nations better understand the Leahy process and their own responsibilities in it. Moreover, such conversations encourage dialogue with partner nations on human rights practices and provide the U.S. government with an opportunity to encourage improvement on the partner nation's human rights performance. As the case of Colombia demonstrates, a partner nation committed to the Leahy process and well versed in its requirements and procedures can achieve remarkable success. There is probably no better example of cooperation in Leahy vetting than Colombia, which is particularly remarkable, given Colombia's troubled human rights record during much of the late 20th century. Colombia did not become a model of cooperation by accident. It was the result of many years of clear guidance and proactive planning by officials in both DoS and DoD.

Recommendations

The Leahy vetting process is a bureaucratic tool—but a tool with a clear policy purpose: improved respect for human rights from U.S. partner security forces. These recommendations address ways that directly or indirectly improve DoD's capacity and capability for implementing the Leahy laws more efficiently and effectively, but they are only useful to the extent that they advance the core goal of Leahy vetting.

Overall: Establish Strategic Working Groups

Officials from DoS and DoD are extremely dedicated to implementing the Leahy laws, with one DoS official noting that any stakeholder in the Leahy process is encouraged to call at any time with concerns. Nevertheless, our analysis indicated that effective and efficient implementation is hampered by a process that needs to be more interactive and transparent. To help address these concerns, we recommend that DoS and DoD establish four working groups for DoD Leahy law issues: Process, Case Determination, Training and Staffing, and Partner Relationships. These working groups would replace and expand upon the current Incident Review Team structure and include representatives from DoS DRL, regional and other bureaus, OSD, the Joint Staff, and CCMD officials. National Security Council staff could also be empowered to participate directly in these working groups to help resolve differences and increase visibility on the issues. These representatives would meet regularly to discuss ways to improve every aspect of implementation, get ahead of problems, and resolve outstanding cases and complaints from stakeholders. Each working group would be coordinated by one DoS and one DoD official, who would serve as sources of information and process improvement facilitators. They would facilitate strategic engagement by OSD and DoS DRL in significant security-assistance planning efforts before the vetting process has begun, so that DoS and DoD human rights stakeholders can help shape these efforts, rather than manage them in an assembly-line fashion. To ensure the lead offices in OSD and DRL maintain strong leadership positions across their organizations on these issues, they could report regularly—perhaps quarterly—to the Under Secretary of State for Civilian Security, Democracy, and Human Rights and the Under Secretary of Defense for Policy

Given staffing constraints, it is important to note that individual officials could serve on multiple working groups, and while meetings should be systematic, they would not need to be frequent. For example, rather than four OSD officials each co-leading a weekly working group, two officials could run two groups each that meet monthly. The goal would not be to dramatically increase the number of meetings but rather to establish more structured, regularized, and strategic interactions and thereby improve communication between DoD and DoS and between Washington and the field. As part of this working group structure, DoD and DoS could develop a more mature personnel exchange process with, for example, a DoD element serving full time at DoS DRL but reporting to OSD.

Overall: Establish a Few Country-Specific Sub–Working Groups

For embassies with less than perhaps a 95-percent approval rate for Leahy-vetting cases, we recommend that DoS DRL and OSD establish sub–working groups that report to the Case Determination Working Group proposed above. These groups would supplement the more assembly line–like structure that tends to suffice for most embassies. Sub–working groups would require additional staff time to allow more-robust discussions at embassies and among staffs at embassies, CCMDs, OSD, the Joint Staff, and DoS headquarters but, in the long run, should result in better prepared and informed stakeholders, fewer misunderstandings, and clearer outcomes. Up-front time investments would likely be offset through reduction of wasted time and growth of productive time.

Process: Partially Standardize Embassy SOPs

As discussed in Chapter Two, we found the clarity and comprehensiveness of SOPs varied widely among embassies. While it would be counterproductive to apply the same SOP to every embassy, we recommend that DoS DRL and OSD—through the Process Working Group recommended above—help embassies partially standardize their SOPs through the use of some template language. The Working Group could review existing SOPs to identify the clearest, most comprehensive SOP language, as well as best practices, and create template language from the components that could apply universally to all SOPs. Best practices could be institutionalized for such issues as relationship building, internal coordination mechanisms, proactive management of vetting requests, streamlining processes to obtain partner-nation information, DI searches, and remediation approaches.

Process: Improve Vetting Transparency Through INVEST

We recommend that DoS and DoD revise Leahy vetting guidance to require stakeholders at every level to document in much greater detail the deliberations and decisions during each step of the process. This could be done by requiring vetters to provide this information consistently in the note section of each case file, as well as through a mandatory drop-down field that would appear when a case is rejected, suspended, or canceled. Nonapproval notes in INVEST already provide some explanation of why a final decision was made, but the level of detail and number of people inputting relevant information could be expanded, which would provide a fuller picture of discussions that took place. Guidance could also require that embassy SOPs highlight exactly how DoD and other stakeholders can engage in each of these steps.

Process: Improve DoD Access to INVEST

We recommend that DoS provide a way for DoD stakeholders who do not have DoS badges to access information in INVEST more easily.

Ideally, this could be done by allowing access to INVEST through DoD Common Access Cards, through a password-protection system, or—at a minimum—through the establishment of at least one dedicated INVEST terminal for each CCMD, OSD, and the Joint Staff. The Process Working Group proposed above could evaluate the costs and benefits of various options.

Process: Enable INVEST to Better Support High-Level Analysis

Although we found relatively little anecdotal evidence that Leahy-vetting challenges were resulting in significant numbers of training cancellations, we were surprised that there is currently no way to analyze this question quantitatively without requiring a time-consuming case-by-case aggregation of the data in INVEST and at individual embassies around the world. We found the same challenge would hinder efforts to aggregate Title 10 cases separately from Title 22 cases. We recommend DoS and DoD work together to improve INVEST's ability to support high-level analysis of how case determinations affect training events, as well as analysis of Title 10 cases and events in aggregate.

Process: Supplement Leahy Remediation Guidance and Provide Support to Remediation Efforts

Although DoD stakeholders expressed gratitude that remediation guidance now exists, there was also a widely held feeling that the path to rehabilitation was confusing and difficult. Rehabilitation guidance that is rarely used will prove to be a wasted opportunity to broaden the influence of the Leahy laws. Thus, we recommend that the Process Working Group hold a series of small remediation workshops with a range of U.S. government stakeholders to discuss the goals, costs, benefits, and risks of remediation in a strategic context. The workshops could also provide a forum for implementers (e.g., embassy staff from Bogota and Mexico City) to share their experiences and develop best practices. The working group might also produce informal guidance (e.g., frequently asked questions [FAQs]) to supplement formal guidance, as a way of helping wary stakeholders take the first steps and thus make remediation a more viable and meaningful option for more partners.

In previous RAND research on standing up new processes in DoD, we have found it useful for process owners to understand and communicate that the system will not be perfect from the start, and that stakeholders at multiple levels (e.g., implementation, planning, policy) need to participate in the process to iterate, streamline, and strengthen the system.[13] CCMDs that have not benefitted from remediation efforts might nominate and support one or two "test cases" in collaboration with the working group. this would not only improve the current process but also allow stakeholders to share information in real time about how the process works and encourage more of them to pursue remediation efforts for relevant units. We have also found that evaluations are an essential component of learning in new processes.[14] Therefore, we recommend that the Leahy Process Working Group should evaluate remediation efforts to document best practices.

Process: Track Cases Persistently

We recommend that the Process Working Group develop a simple database to track Leahy vetting cases that are approved but that subsequently face accusations for acts either prior or subsequent to their vetting. Whenever accusations of human rights violations arise in a country, embassy staff could check names of accused individuals and units against INVEST data to identify whether previously approved cases might be implicated. These new accusations would then be researched via the same vetting procedures used for all cases. INVEST could have an additional column to note whether an approved, suspended, or canceled case is subsequently found to have committed violations, whether that was before or after a determination had been made.

This revetting would likely involve a short list of cases (we found little evidence this is an issue) but could be valuable for enhancing

---

[13] See, for example, Michael J. McNerney, Jefferson P. Marquis, S. Rebecca Zimmerman, and Ariel Klein, *SMART Security Cooperation Objectives: Improving DoD Planning and Guidance*, Santa Monica, Calif.: RAND Corporation, RR-1430-OSD, 2016.

[14] See Jefferson P. Marquis, Michael J. McNerney, S. Rebecca Zimmerman, Merrie Archer, Jeremy Boback, and David Stebbins, *Developing an Assessment, Monitoring and Evaluation Framework for Department of Defense Security Cooperation*, Santa Monica, Calif.: RAND Corporation, RR-1611-OSD, 2016.

transparency and trust in the system and helping DoS and DoD learn from potential mistakes. It would strengthen the influence of the Leahy-vetting process on human rights efforts by making the Leahy vetting more persistent, i.e., by recognizing that the tracking of DI does not end just because a case is approved.

Time Lines: For DoD Leahy Law Cases, Add a "Second Review" Step to the Vetting Process

As discussed earlier, suspensions and cancellations play an important role in the Leahy vetting process, but based on our analysis of how many of these cases are determined, we believe their current rate (approximately 9 percent) indicates a suboptimal process, with too many cases set aside without final resolution. While some interviewees believed that this approach helped keep the process running smoothly, others argued that suspensions and cancellations create confusion among vetters and partners alike, additional challenges for DoD planners, time pressures as planners scramble to substitute one set of individuals and units for others, and resentment among partners. Thus, we recommend that DoS and DoD add a second, five-day review process to the end of the vetting timetable for DoD Leahy-law cases to allow the Case Determination Working Group to conduct additional research and discussion of cases with "preliminary" suspensions or cancellations. This will require vetters to submit cases slightly earlier than the current guidance directs, thus easing the pressures that sometimes erupt and allowing more time for open deliberation. After this new process step has been established and assessed, DoS and DoD could set a goal to reduce suspensions and cancellations, perhaps by a significant percentage, since the new process should make vetting more effective and with clearer outcomes.

Clarity of Scope: Address Real World Frequently Asked Questions

Although we found the guidance explaining what programs require Leahy vetting to be relatively clear, it is also true that implementing such guidance in the real world can still be challenging in some cases. Thus, we recommend two steps. OSD should update its guidance and supplement it with informal guidance that helps address real-world questions and scenarios to illustrate and help vetters think through how they are applying this guidance. For example, informal guidance could discuss in plain language how the line between activities that do not require vetting (e.g., familiarization and interoperability) and those that do (e.g., training and other assistance) can sometimes be blurry and what, therefore, planners can do to clarify their intent. Informal guidance could also discuss how posts sometimes use the Leahy-vetting process to implement policy decisions that are not required by law. For example, some posts take a "vet everything" approach, which can be a proactive and effective way to use an existing system to advance other policy goals or to go beyond the letter of the Leahy laws to embrace the spirit of the laws. Much of this additional guidance could be developed in the form of FAQs, which can be a very useful method of informally imparting real-world knowledge.

Information Used: Make Determinations More Transparent

We recommend that DoS and DoD use the Case Determination Working Group to more transparently and inclusively deliberate over what information is determined to be credible and what is not, particularly as stakeholders argued that the existing Incident Review Team process has proven inadequate. The group could either leverage INVEST or develop a simple database to track these determinations, which will help document past case experience and thereby benefit future deliberations. Because effective case determinations are central to effective Leahy implementation, greater collaboration and transparency in determining the credibility of DI would likely help prevent or resolve many other Leahy-vetting challenges.

Training and Staff Resources: Improve Formal and Informal Training

Given the weaknesses we found in staff training, we have two recommendations. First, we recommend that the Training Working Group assess and document the formal training requirements for various participants in the Leahy-vetting process. Specifically, the group should identify several categories of staff and what kinds of training they require, e.g., activity planners, vetters, overseers. They should also identify formal training sources and how to access those sources. Second, we recommend the group create an online annotated briefing to supplement formal training. Like the FAQ list we recommend earlier, this annotated briefing could include a more broad-ranging FAQ section, regularly updated based on real-world questions from stakeholders. The last slide of this briefing would include a link to the DoS and DoD working group coordinators, who could answer questions that aren't already covered in the FAQ section. Although this effort will require dedicated staff time, it should reduce staffing challenges across the Leahy-vetting system over time, because staff experts will be more efficient in their work and other staff will be able to more effectively support the staff expert when he or she is unavailable or overwhelmed.

Training and Staff Resources: Establish a Human Rights Coordinator at Every CCMD

For implementation of the Leahy laws to be strategically managed and well integrated with security assistance planning, the CCMDs should play a proactive role. While not every CCMD requires a multiperson office to do this, we recommend that each CCMD at least have a human rights coordinator with responsibilities for promoting human rights awareness among regional partners and CCMD and embassy staff, improving implementation of the DoS and DoD Leahy laws, and facilitating security cooperation planning. We recommend the coordinator serve in this role full time at all the CCMDs, except perhaps for U.S. European Command, which might require only a half-time position. Although CCMD staffs were downsizing in 2015 and 2016, it appeared that the long-term benefits we observed at USSOUTH-COM of a human rights coordinator were well worth the opportunity costs and would apply quite well to DoD's other CCMDs: fewer deadline pressures, better understanding of the laws and related policies, clearer internal and external communication, improved timetables, more satisfactory adjudication, better training, and reduced tensions with partners.

Partner Relationships: Improve Communication Guidance and Support

We recommend the Partner Relationships Working Group hold a series of small workshops similar to the remediation workshops proposed earlier to better understand the challenges and best practices associated with engaging partners in Leahy-vetting and human rights discussions. The group could document best practices identified by various embassies, including major success stories (e.g., Colombia) and current challenging environments (e.g., Mexico and Nigeria), as well as embassies with fewer challenges but nevertheless helpful tips (e.g., Mongolia). Once the group has strengthened its understanding of challenges and best practices, it could develop robust guidance for how stakeholders should communicate with partners, as well as how to communicate internally to develop partner engagement strategies and externally to strengthen consultation with partner-nation citizens and civil-society organizations.

Abbreviations

APRI	Asia Pacific Regional Initiative
CCMD	combatant command
CRS	Congressional Research Service
DI	derogatory information
DISAM	Defense Institute of Security Assistance Management (now Institute of Security Cooperation Studies)
DoD	Department of Defense
DoS	Department of State
DRL	Department of State Bureau of Democracy, Human Rights and Labor
FAQ	frequently asked question
FY	fiscal year
GAO	U.S. Government Accountability Office
GVHR	gross violation of human rights
INVEST	International Vetting and Security Tracking
ISCS	Institute of Security Cooperation Studies (formerly Defense Institute of Security Assistance Management)

NGO	nongovernmental organization
SECDEF	Secretary of Defense
SOP	standard operating procedure
TCA	Traditional CCMD Activities
USC	U.S. Code
USNORTHCOM	U.S. Northern Command
USSOUTHCOM	U.S. Southern Command

References

The Antideficiency Act, PL 97–258, 96 Stat. 923.

Cadei, Emily, "Foreign Militaries, Domestic Tension," *CQ Weekly*, December 16, 2013.

Carl Levin and Howard P. "Buck" McKeon National Defense Authorization Act for Fiscal Year 2015, PL 113-291, December 19, 2014. As of June 27, 2016: https://www.congress.gov/113/plaws/publ291/PLAW-113publ291.pdf

Center for International Policy, Security Assistance Monitor website, undated. As of October 28, 2015: http://securityassistance.org

Consolidated Appropriations Act, 2012, PL 112-74, December 23, 2011. As of June 27, 2016: https://www.gpo.gov/fdsys/pkg/PLAW-112publ74/pdf/PLAW-112publ74.pdf

Consolidated Appropriations Act, 2014, PL 113-76, January 17, 2014. As of June 27, 2016: https://www.gpo.gov/fdsys/pkg/PLAW-113publ76/pdf/PLAW-113publ76.pdf

Defense Institute of Security Assistance Management, *DISAM's Online Green Book: The Management of Security Assistance*, 2007–2008. As of September 30, 2016: http://www.ISCS.dsca.mil/pubs/DR/greenbook.htm

DoD—*See* U.S. Department of Defense.

DoS—*See* U.S. Department of State.

DRL—*See* U.S. Department of State, Bureau of Democracy, Human Rights and Labor.

Egozi, Sara, "Aid Is Key to Reform Local Forces on Rights, Leahy Says," Washington, D.C.: United States Institute of Peace, February 12, 2016. As of September 30, 2016: http://www.usip.org/olivebranch/2016/02/12/aid-key-reform-local-forces-rights-leahy-says

Foreign Assistance Act of 1961, Public Law 87-195, as amended through PL 114–195, enacted July 20, 2016. As of June 27, 2016:
http://legcounsel.house.gov/Comps/Foreign%20Assistance%20Act%20Of%201961.pdf

Foreign Operations, Export Financing, and Related Programs Appropriations Act, 1998, PL 105-118, November 26, 1997. As of June 27, 2016:
http://uscode.house.gov/statutes/pl/105/118.pdf

GAO—See U.S. Government Accountability Office.

Gillison, Douglas, "Moral Hazard: How the United States Trained Cambodian Human Rights Abusers, Breaking U.S. Law," 100 Reporters website, March 18, 2016. As of September 30, 2016:
https://100r.org/2016/03/moral-hazard-how-the-united-states-trained-cambodian-human-rights-abusers-breaking-u-s-law/

Ham, Linwood, "Human Rights Violations: U.S. Foreign Aid Accountability and Prevention," Washington, D.C.: United States Institute of Peace, March 29, 2015. As of September 30, 2016:
http://www.usip.org/olivebranch/2015/03/29/human rights-violations-us-foreign-aid-accountability-and-prevention

Joint Staff, "Human Rights Verification for DoD-Funded Training of Foreign Personnel," policy message, DTG071300Z, June 2004.

Marquis, Jefferson P., Michael J. McNerney, S. Rebecca Zimmerman, Merrie Archer, Jeremy Boback, and David Stebbins, *Developing an Assessment, Monitoring and Evaluation Framework for Department of Defense Security Cooperation*, Santa Monica, Calif.: RAND Corporation, RR-1611-OSD, 2016. As of October 18, 2016:
http://www.rand.org/pubs/research_reports/RR1611.html

McNerney, Michael J., Jefferson P. Marquis, S. Rebecca Zimmerman, and Ariel Klein, *SMART Security Cooperation Objectives: Improving DoD Planning and Guidance*, Santa Monica, Calif.: RAND Corporation, RR-1430-OSD, 2016. As of October 3, 2016:
http://www.rand.org/pubs/research_reports/RR1430.html

Mudge, Lewis, "The Executioners' Bill," Human Rights Watch website, March 26, 2015. As of October 18, 2016:
https://www.hrw.org/news/2015/03/26/executioners-bill

Office of the Secretary of Defense, guidance memo, August 18, 2014, Not available to the general public.

Ruble, Kayla, "Nigerian President Blames US Human Rights Law for 'Aiding and Abetting' Boko Haram," Vice News website, July 23, 2015. As of September 30, 2016:
https://news.vice.com/article/nigerian-president-blames-us-human-rights-law-for-aiding-and-abetting-boko-haram

Serafino, Nina M., June S. Beittel, Lauren Ploch Blanchard, and Liana Rosen, *"Leahy Law" Human Rights Provisions and Security Assistance: Issue Overview*, Washington, D.C.: Congressional Research Service, R43361, January 29, 2014. As of June 27, 2016:
https://www.fas.org/sgp/crs/row/R43361.pdf

Striffolino, Kathryn R., and Nate Smith, "Deconstructing Leahy Law: Fact vs Fiction," Amnesty International website, July 9, 2013. As of September 30, 2016:
http://blog.amnestyusa.org/africa/deconstructing-the-leahy-law-fact-vs-fiction

Toosi, Nahal, "State Dept. Assures Leahy on Israeli Human Rights Scrutiny," Politico website, May 5, 2016. As of September 30, 2016:
http://www.politico.com/story/2016/05/
state-department-israel-human-rights-scrutiny-222734

USAID, "The Greenbook," website, April 29, 2013. As of October 18, 2016:
https://www.usaid.gov/developer/greenbookapi

U.S. Code, Title 10, §2249e, Prohibition on use of funds for assistance to units of foreign security forces that have committed a gross violation of human rights (Added Pub. L. 113–291, div. A, title XII, § 1204(a)(1), Dec. 19, 2014, 128 Stat. 3531)

U.S. Code, Title 22, §2378d, Limitation on assistance to security forces, current through Pub. L. 114-38

U.S. Congress, "Human Rights Vetting: Nigeria and Beyond," hearing before the Subcommittee on Africa, Global Health, Global Human Rights, and International Organizations, Committee on Foreign Affairs, House of Representatives, 113th Cong., 2nd Sess., July 10, 2014. As of September 30, 2016:
https://www.gpo.gov/fdsys/pkg/CHRG-113hhrg88627/html/CHRG-
113hhrg88627.htm

U.S. Department of Defense, "Report for Fiscal Year 2014 in Response to Section 1204(b) of the Carl Levin and Howard P. 'Buck' McKeon National Defense Authorization Act for Fiscal Year 2015, Public Law 113-291," March 31, 2015.

———, "Report for Fiscal Year 2015 in Response to Section 1204(b) of the Carl Levin and Howard P. 'Buck' McKeon National Defense Authorization Act for Fiscal Year 2015," Public Law 113-291, March 31, 2016.

U.S. Department of Defense and U.S. Department of State, "The Joint Department of Defense and DoS Policy on Remediation and the Resumption of Assistance Under the Leahy Laws," February 2015.

U.S. Department of State, *Foreign Affairs Manual*, website, undated. As of September 30, 2016:
https://fam.state.gov/

———, "Compliance with the State and DoD Leahy Laws: A Guide to Vetting Policy & Process," Washington, D.C., September 2012.

————, "Leahy Vetting: Law, Policy, Process," briefing slides, Washington, D.C., April 15, 2013. As of September 30, 2016:
http://www.humanrights.gov/wp-content/uploads/2011/10/leahy-vetting-law-policy-and-process.pdf

U.S. Government, Foreign Assistance website (beta), undated. As of October 18, 2016:
http://foreignassistance.gov/

U.S. Government Accountability Office, "Human Rights: Additional Guidance, Monitoring, and Training Could Improve Implementation of the Leahy Laws," Washington, D.C., GAO-13-866, September 2013. As of June 27, 2016:
http://www.gao.gov/products/GAO-13-866

————, "Security Assistance: U.S. Government Should Strengthen End-Use Monitoring and Human Rights Vetting for Egypt," Washington, D.C., GAO-16-435, April 2016. As of June 27, 2016:
http://www.gao.gov/products/GAO-16-435

Womack, David, "Human Rights Vetting: The Process and Lessons Learned," *ISCS Journal*, July 2007.